HOLISTIC PSYCHOLOGY OF ALEXANDER PINT

# GRATITUDE FOR THE REQUEST OF THE SOUL

### BY ALEXANDER PINT

Translated by Emin Kuliev, MD
www.pint.ru
https://caterpillartobuterfly.wordpress.com

**Visit www.SkyrocketPress.com**

Cover art by Freydoon Rassouli
ISBN: 978-1-944722-06-7

# TABLE OF CONTENTS

•▶◀•▶◀•▶◀•▶◀•▶◀•▶◀•▶◀•▶◀•▶◀•▶◀•▶◀•▶◀•

# CHAPTER 1
# A HUMAN BEING AS A PHARMACEUTICAL FACTORY

•◆•◆•◆•◆•◆•◆•◆•◆•◆•◆•◆•◆•◆•◆•◆•◆•◆•◆•

## What brought you to meet Pint?

— Good morning. I will ask those of you who are here for the first time to tell us about yourselves.

— *I have been suffering from anxiety and depresion for five years. I had to take Xanax and Prozac for many years. I have seen many psychotherapists and psychiatrists to no avail. I found your site on the "Self-knowledge" site that I visit from time to time, so I listened to your webinar, and here I am.*

— What are the key words here? You mentioned "Self-knowledge". What did you react to exactly?

— *I am not sure what I reacted to. I probably reacted to your explanation that emotions, such as condemnation and guilt, are narcotics. I feel these emotions all the time. I constantly blame and condemn people around me. I condemn myself too.*

— So, condemnation is something with which you are very familiar; you know this state very well.

— *I got very interested in your idea of a dual nature of personality. I spend a lot of time thinking about why certain events occur. We think we create what we want. I could never understand why I want to create what I create.*

— Okay. As I understand it, you have experienced this inner misbalance to quite a strong degree. You mentioned that you have seen psychologists and psychiatrists. What did they offer you? Did they help you?

— *My last psychotherapist told me my self-esteem was too low. I did not develop it during childhood. He suggested I work on it.*

— Great! Inner self-assuredness. He recommended that you work on your inner self-assuredness. And how did he explain why you lack it?

— *He said it was caused by extensive parental criticism during childhood. My parents were too critical. They never supported me. They never praised me. I was always afraid to make a mistake.*

— He thought that your anxiety was due to parental condemnation, and he advised you to work on it and to get rid of it. How did he suggest you do that?

— *He did not offer anything concrete. I spent two hours a week talking to him. It did not last long because it did not lead anywhere.*

— But he talked, and he talked well, right? This is modern psychology. People get diplomas and collect money for practicing it.

So, what is the reason you are anxious all the time? Is this your primary state?

— *Yes, this is the state I am in most of the time. I feel constantly split. I constantly argue with myself. I want to do something, but on the other hand, I do not want to do it. I am being torn to pieces. In the end, I become hysterical. I sit down, and I do not do anything.*

— In the end, you have no power. This inner conflict consumes all your energy. You fight this fight, exhaust yourself, and sit down to rest. What exactly do you fight about? Which part of you is fighting? You have many different parts within you. I want to talk to the part that is fighting this fight.

— *Well, I have to go to work. However, I frequently do not feel well. I am also afraid to make a mistake. On top of that, I am sort of married. Not sort of, I am married.*

— I am married, and I sort of have a husband.

*— He does not ask anything from me, but I live with the constant feeling that I owe him something. For example, why does he work, but I don't? Why don't I clean and tidy up our apartment? I constantly feel guilty. It is so strange. I even feel guilty about my cat. We have a cat, and I feel guilty for not feeding it on time, for not petting it enough. This is crazy! Sometimes, I feel like I want to go and get a job, but the more I want it, the more I doubt that I really want it. I get headaches because of it, and I get very anxious. I want it badly, and I should do something. That is the way it is. I cannot go right, and I cannot go left. I get angry with myself.*

— Let's take a look at your situation. You said, "I am sort of married. I sort of have a husband." This is not an accidental phrase. It is easier to live with that sort of an agenda. You look at him: sort of a husband. You look at yourself: sort of a wife. However, you are not a hundred percent wife; you do not have to clean up today. If you are a wife, you are always a wife. However, in your case, today— a wife, but tomorrow—not a wife. When I will be your wife, I will do it. Currently, I do not know, we "kind of live together."

*— That's what I constantly experience. For example, I think I am kind of sick now.*

— Kind of?

*— Yes, I am kind of sick now. That is why I am not going to do anything now. I am not going to spend much effort because I will not be able to do anything well now, while I must do everything very well and show everyone how good I am. So, I had better wait. When I am better, I will…*

— And for now, I will live—sort of live. We think we live while, in reality, we "sort of live." This is very interesting. So, what does this roller-coaster experience of "want—don't want" offer you? You are dealing with a certain state that manifests itself in action.  You get ready to have a job interview, but you do not do it. You get ready to wash the dishes, but you do not do it. However, something happens during this time. Something happens on the emotional level that offers you a certain experience. What happens exactly? And what are you holding on to so strongly, though you do not even understand it? You would rather get better, but in reality, your problem continues. This provides you with something very important. What is it?

# Who is hiding there?

— *I am afraid to make a mistake. I am kind of afraid to be seen in a bad light. Here it comes again, "kind of, sort of!"*

— Great. The phrase ***kind of*** is the key!

— *I have a feeling that if I were to show myself in a bad way somewhere, I would not be able to change the impression I have created. I am afraid of it. Perhaps this inner conflict and anxiety provide me with an opportunity to not do anything.*

— Yes, but take a look here. You are constantly occupied. In addition, the business in which you are involved is a great business. You are constantly anxious. What are you anxious about? You have just said, "I may show myself in a bad way. I may create a bad impression. I may appear in a bad light."

— *I am not good enough.*

— You are not good enough. We are dealing with a certain reference number here. Let us consider how it plays out here, in our setting. You want to be good here, too. What does it mean to be good here, right now?

— *I don't know.*

— But you are trying to create this impression, nevertheless.

— *I apraise my apearance when I get out of the house. I put on lipstick and mascara. I have to be presentable externally.*

— You have to look good. This is rule number one.

— *I have to look good. I have to create the appearance of a smart, good looking, and open human being. I am afraid to appear stupid.*

— What else? What other impression, aside from what you have already mentioned, do you want me to have of you?

— *I don't know.*

— What would happen if I were to tell you that you look bad or stupid, and that you should not even be here? Look. I have already said that.

— *I dont like it.*

— You agree with what I said, and as a result of you agreeing with it, you get upset. If you did not consider yourself as such, you would have said, "Pint is getting old. He is turning into an idiot." Therefore, that is who you consider yourself to be. Though you consider yourself to be bad and stupid, you do not want to show yourself as such. You hide yourself. So, why do you hide yourself, and who in you is trying to hide?

— *I hide myself.*

— Who is that *you* who hides? The one who hides is also you. Look. You hide yourself from yourself. Why?

— *I want to believe I am a good person. It seems to me that I am a good person.*

— So, you want to think of yourself as a good person. Therefore, you need to hide this bad one and keep her in the dark. In that case, you only show one side of a coin to the people around you. On the other side, you are the opposite. Moreover, you do not show that side to anyone. That is what makes you anxious and depressed all the time. You are thinking, "What if that other side were to show itself?"

# How a child fails to fulfill the expectations of his parents

*— There is something else here. Not only am I afraid to show this side of me to others, I am also afraid to look in that direction myself.*

— Exactly. You have a fear of seeing and manifesting this side of yourself. Where did you get this fear? Someone instilled it in you "Don't look there!" Who used to say that?

*— It was Mom. My mother was rough. "You should not get nervous! You should not cry! Pull yourself together and don't bother me!" I am not sure why, but she used to repeat the phrase "No one needs you." I would come home and ask her, "Did anyone call me?" She would answer, "No. No one needs you."*

— But she, your mother, she needed you, right?

*— Yes, she needed me.*

— And why did she need you?

*— By the way, Mom always wanted a girl. I have a brother who is ten years my senior, and all those years she wanted a girl. She is a mathematician, and she always wanted me to follow in her footsteps. My brother was not a problem child. He was always the quiet type. I, on the other hand, turned out to be very active. I could never sit still. That irritated her.*

— What exactly irritated her?

*— She was irritated by my acting out and not being obedient enough.*

— Was it your state that irritated her, or the fact that you didn't follow certain norms?

*— I don't know. I was just a young child at the time. Then there came adolescent rebellion. I decided to pursue an acting career. She was against it. She expected me to be a mathematician. We argued nonstop throughout my high school years. She used to say, "Who needs you there? Take a look at yourself."*

— Who needs you but math?

— *By the way, she still laments that I am wasting a great mathematical mind.*

— Okay. Here is your duality: math, logic, and the mind are masculine attributes, while acting and feelings are feminine. We are dealing with the heart and the mind here.

— *Dad almost never interfered, but when I decided to become a model, he looked at me skeptically and said, "This is not for people like you."*

— And who is it for?

— *I am not that tall. I am not fat, but I am not skinny either. Perhaps he did not find me pretty enough. Models should be beautiful and skinny.*

— Coat hangers.

— *Yes, tall and beautiful coat hangers. My family was upset that I was trying to make myself look beautiful by spending hours in front of the mirror and applying make-up. My mom has never used make-up.*

— You wanted to show off. An acting career presupposes that.

— *Yes, I did. I still like to do that.*

— Okay. So where is the shadow side here? Can you show us something out of your shadow side? You are an actress. Can you show us something?

— *That's the thing. I am not that good. I am scared to show myself. I am afraid I will not be able to play the part.*

— An actor should be able to play any role, right?

— *When I act, I can allow myself to look unattractive.*

— Okay. Are you acting now?

— *Right now?*

— What's wrong with that?

— *I dont know. It depends.*

— You can play anything you want here, in our show. Actors can show mastery playing any role. You should be able to play a killer and villain well. Go ahead. Show us something out of your negative assortment. Let us see your darkest sides.

— *My darkest sides? I have been there lately. My parents and my husband have irritated me for a long time. They irritate the hell out of me.*

— What do you want to do?

— *Sometimes I want to hit them on the head with something heavy.*

— Go ahead. Do it. How about some classic roles?

— *Negative roles?*

— Yes, something negative. Raskolnikov killed the old woman. Let's have you play a new version of Raskolnikov, a female version.

— *I always liked Margarita in* Master and Margarita. *She leaves her rich husband and signs a contract with the devil.*

— Don't forget how well she plays the Queen, when every villain comes and kisses her knee.

— *I like that. I like negative roles better.*

— What other roles can you play? How about Lady Macbeth?

# Find a "star" in yourself

— *A couple days ago, we were invited to the premier of a movie. It contained some very graphic, almost pornographic scenes. The actress who played the leading role was a porn star. During the first half of the movie, I thought, "How horrible. I am going to stand up and leave now." However, after a while, I suddenly thought to myself, "Why am I so concerned?" I was able to sit through the entire movie, but I was shaking for the rest of the evening.*

— Why were you shaking?

— *It seems to me that I was looking at myself. It is stupid, but …*

— Would you play that role?

— *Yes, but I would not just play that role. This is in me, and I do not like it.*

— This part should not be brought to light. People should not see it.

— *I felt uncomfortable watching this movie while surrounded by people.*

— You were surrounded by people who, God forbid, could have noticed that you have it in you. Here we go! Tell us about the life of a porn star. Use some episodes from your own life.

— *In that case, I am a pornstar who openly declares to the whole world what she does for a living. My name is Alysia, and I am giving my first interview.*

— And what do they ask her?

— *They ask me what I feel on the set, and whether I find it pleasant or unpleasant. They ask me whether I am ashamed to be filmed in the pornographic movies or not. They ask me if I am ashamed to have sex in front of the camera.*

— Alysia is being asked, "Have you had sex in the Red Square?"— "Yes, I did"— she says, "We were shooting all over Red Square. I had sex in the Mausoleum twice." What do you feel now?

— *I feel good. It feels like a huge weight fell off my shoulders.*

— What else can you do?

— *Oh, I have to have at least ten people watch me have sex. I cannot get sexually aroused without an audience. I invite everyone I know to watch me: friends, neighbors.*

— And what is the plot of this movie?

— *There is no plot. I just have sex in different places.*

— What do you mean, "I just have sex?" Where is the plot? We need to have some naturalism here. What is most important for a porn star: her face or her ass?

— *Her ass is much more important for her.*

— What kind of ass do you have? Is it a philosophical ass? Is it a sad and quiet ass or an ass full of energy? We are interviewing your ass. Our reporter asks your ass now, "What are looking for in life?"

— *I am looking for adventure!*

— Great. "I am looking for adventure!" Can you make this process nobler?

— *I was at a party yesterday where I had to watch a movie about an artistic fart.*

— Did you have to? Were you forced to?

— *Well, everyone was watching. I could not excuse myself.*

— How did you get to this party? Who brought you to the place where people watch these types of movies?

— *It's just ...*

— **See, the holistic point of view does not allow us to think that way. We cannot use the phrase, "It is just happened." As you know by now, nothing happens accidentally, and nothing happens without a reason. If you were shown this movie, you wanted to see it.** You can tell your friends, "I was brought to this room and was forced to watch this movie." Do not tell us that. We know this is not the case.

— *My ass wanted that.*

— *Hmmm, the themes we discuss ...*

— And straight from the get go.

## What is the meaning of perverted pleasure?

— *I was forty years old when I learned about some of the perversions people pay for. Some people come to these places in order to be peed and pooped on. They pay a lot of money to experience that. Special glass tables are being used so other people can observe this.*

— You are quite lucky. Most people die without getting to know these things.

— *I saw it in a movie.*

— Another movie you have been forced to watch, ah?

— *No, I was flipping through the channels one night, and I stumbled across it. It was an interesting movie. It showed the relationship between a man and a woman without any ...*

— Without romance.

— *No, it was actually very romantic. They were high school sweethearts. They loved each other, but they fought all the time. They could not talk about anything without getting into a fight. They grew up, and the girl got tired of fighting. She decided to move to another country to break this relationship. She throws a farewell party before departure, and he finds out about it. He comes to the party wanting to tell her how much he loves her, but he cannot face her. He goes to the restroom to snort a line of cocaine and to gather his courage. He meets some people there. He shares drugs with them, and one of them tells him to be a man and talk to the girl. He replies that he cannot do that.*

— Do we watch this whole scene with him sitting on a toilet?

— *No, of course not. They are in a huge restroom. They stand by the mirror talking. No one is sitting on a toilet. The older guy tells him, "You are a spring chicken. You don't know anything about life yet." He tells him his story. He had become impotent a few years ago, and his wife had left him. He tells the first man what it means to be impotent. He describes what he feels. After he became impotent, he started to go to these places. He has to use different perverted methods to become sexually excited. He cannot do it any other way. The way the movie is shot follows every story he tells graphically.*

— This movie is an apotheosis of love.

— *He describes the prostitutes he goes to and how he chooses them. The movie shows him having sex with two women defecating on him. It was a very interesting movie. It was four in the morning, but I could not stop watching it.*

— We can't stop listening to you.

— *Later on, the young guy got out of the bathroom and, being very emotional, started a fight with his girlfriend.*

— Was he able to relieve his tension through this act?

— *Which act?*

— I am afraid to call it a sex act, but I think that's what it was. It is usually a man who gets relieved, but in this case, it looks like a woman got her relief too. So, what happened to this man at the end?

— *Oh, you mean…?*

11

— Exactly. This is basic. This is the apotheosis of love. She came, and she relieved herself. What happened to him?

— *But she is a prostitute...*

— Wait. I am interested in something else now.

— *He got a certain pleasure out of it too. He went there to get high. When he gets out of the whorehouse, he condemns himself saying, "On my God, what have I come to? What am I doing here?! What do I need this for?" Those are his thoughts. I had the same thought in my head, "Why does he go there?"*

— Why? Isn't it obvious to you? You described everything, and suddenly you ask, "Why?" You have answered this question already.

— *What kind of satisfaction does he get if he condemns himself for what he does?*

— This is his main satisfaction. We have come to the main topic now! Look at the long preparation we had. Finally, we have arrived. What else did he say?

— *He said, "What am I doing here? Why do I come here repeatedly? Do I come here to be defecated on?"*

— And what does he experience in the process?

— *He feels guilt.*

— Yes, he feels the horrific feeling of guilt.

— *Yes, he experiences a horrific feeling of guilt, "What have I come to?!"*

— He experiences a tremendous feeling of guilt, "Why did I come here? I will come here again tomorrow".

— *Yes, I think he goes there not only to experience this perverted sex. That was not what was so exciting for him. He also experiences terrible pain by being there. At one point, he says that the best kaif\** (\* Kaif or Kif - from Arabic kayf pleasure. Any drug or agent that when smoked is capable of producing a euphoric condition. The euphoric condition produced by smoking marijuana) *he ever experienced was associated with being tied down to the point of immobility, with his penis pinned.*

— In that case, he experiences himself as a woman.

12

— *Perhaps he does, but at the same time, he blames and condemns his wife for leaving him, as his degradation started afterwards.*

— "I can't have decent sex with you. I am leaving." Now he understands what is awaiting him. He experiences a strong feeling of guilt.

— *He also experiences physical pain.*

— Yes. Look, we all know what physical pain is. How about emotional pain? What is it?

— *Emotional pain is a state.*

— **What kind of a state? Use a word to describe it. Look, he descends to the apotheosis of guilt. The level of guilt he experiences is staggering. Why does he need that? What is he getting out of it? It is the feeling of guilt he is getting high on. The feeling of guilt is the narcotic he uses! Moreover, he has to escalate the dose all the time.**

— *Yes, next time he will ask these prostitutes to hurt him more. Hmmm, I was watching this movie thinking, "Why does he go there?" I understand why he does it now.*

— *The condemnation is another narcotic, but it carries the opposite sign, right?*

— Exactly. To experience guilt, you must experience condemnation. Our parents provided us with a heavy load of condemnation in childhood. They condemned us and everything around us. What gets fixated in us in such a case? They condemn, and what did we do?

— *I feel guilty.*

— Exactly. You felt guilty, and you start to condemn in return. After a while, guilt transfers into condemnation, because you cannot withstand it any longer. The level of narcotic gets to the limit of your current tolerance level. You will have to elevate this threshold. To do that, you will need even stronger condemnation; you will search for it. This is the narcotic we have all been addicted to since childhood.

— *Does the husband condemn too?*

— *No, the husband keeps repeating, "You are the best. You are my ideal woman. Everything is great," while I say, "No! I don't want you!"*

— "You are not a husband to me!" That is what we need love for.

— *If he were to say something opposite, there would be resistance.*

— Yes, of course.

# The mechanism people use to receive emotional pleasure

— So this is exactly what you need. You want to experience this state: I am not pretty, I am not smart, etc. You have a whole set of these adjectives. What do you feel when someone tells you that you are not pretty? You feel guilt. Everyone who says this to you injects you with a dose of a narcotic. Someone injects you with a higher dose, and someone with a smaller dose, and until you accumulate the dose you need, you are not going to relax. You search for this state of guilt as a drug junky searches for heroin. You search for it like an alcoholic searches for his next drink. Russian style. What is half a bottle of vodka to you? It is nothing. You need it just to get yourself going. Let us drink more. Let us drink until we cannot see straight. Look, this is what you need.

You come here for treatment. What for? This is your basic narcotic. In reality, you do not want to get better. You want to prolong and escalate this state. Your psychotherapist tells you, "Increase your self-esteem, and everything is going to be fine." However, in reality, you do not need that. On the contrary, you need to lower it for the feeling of guilt to get thrown overboard. That is what you want! It **appears** to you that you want to get rid of it. Yet you do not want to do that, because that is how you get your main pleasure.

— *I don't consciously experience the state of guilt as pleasurable. I do not feel it as pleasant. I experience kaif when I condemn someone. Condemnation is a great feeling, but when I experience guilt … I can mentally agree that I need it, but it is painful. It is so painful …*

— This is precisely the pain you need. Behind your physical and emotional pain is guilt.

— *I hurt when someone says something to me about him … I lived with him for ten years and now he is gone… This heavy feeling comes … I am on the verge of tears. I have to go outside and cry. I am all guilt and condemnation. I condemn myself. Then, I immediately feel guilty and start to cry. I was next to him, but I could not save him. I am bad. I am so bad. However, the next thing you know, I have a smile on my face, "Take a look at me. I am actually pretty good." First, I cry. Then I smile. Where is this smile coming from?*

— This is the evil smile. Look, you need to experience this, and you will receive a certain relief. A drug addict runs around until he gets his fix. He is miserable. As soon as he gets his dose, he falls asleep. You have just told us about the moment when you fall asleep. As soon as you felt the drug injected into your vein, a smile appeared on your face: "I am such a bitch!" That is how this drug works. How do you escalate the dose? You do it by condemning yourself.

Let us look at how each one of you condemns yourself and for what exactly you condemn yourself. Each one of you have developed a certain habitual method to procure these narcotics. You do not need to think anymore. You have people near you around whom you feel guilty. You just need to reinforce this state and bring it to the level you need. This is Human Mechanics 101.

*— And personality or ego creates life scenarios to bring you back into this state again and again.*

— Exactly. You keep repeating the same thing again and again. You were hooked on this drug, and you cannot get off it. You do not know how.

*— How about the feelings of shame, humiliation, and resentment? Is guilt also behind them?*

— We need to sort this out in detail. For example, you are ashamed of yourself. What is that mean? In what particular situations do you experience shame?

*— I experience shame when I do something bad.*

— Describe these situations and be very specific.

*— I experience shame when I don't know how to handle my work.*

— Okay. Guilty! What does it mean to be guilty? You have done something in the way it was not supposed to be done. Do you feel guilty for that? **You will see that behind all these words—shame, humiliation, and resentment—is guilt.** Let us look at resentment. Do you feel resentment toward yourself or toward someone else? What do you feel when your resentment is directed toward someone: condemnation or guilt?

*— When I feel resentment toward someone I also feel self-pity.*

— Look, there is condemnation there. When you feel resentment toward someone, it means he did something wrong, and you condemn him for that. However, **if you remember the axiom of the School of Holistic Psychology that there are no other people but you, and that in condemning someone, in reality, you condemn yourself.** In this case, you feel guilt or self-pity. Either you feel guilty or you pity yourself.

*— In my case, I condemn someone, and then I condemn myself for condemning him.*

— Exactly.

— *How about the feeling of humiliation?*

— It depends on how you look at it. When you feel humiliated, you may also feel guilty and blame yourself for doing something wrong. In that case, you feel guilty for providing someone with an opportunity to humiliate you. On the other hand, you can feel self-pity for being humiliated.

— *Behind humiliation is probably a feeling of shame.*

— Okay. What is shame? It is guilt. Irrespective of what you look at, in the end you will arrive at **guilt and pity on one side and condemnation on the other side**. Let us sort it out in detail. We need to sort this out very well.

— *What about the feeling of worthlessness?*

— Okay. You are experiencing the feeling of worthlessness. You are worthless. Why do you experience this feeling?

— *I drove on a freeway for the first time yesterday. I almost got into an accident. Interestingly enough, I did not experience any thoughts, feelings, or states at the time. Only afterwards, when I recalled the event, did I observe this thought: "What would have happened if I had gotten into an accident?" I felt this self-condemnation. I kept thinking about it for a long time.*

— Okay, you are thinking. What about feelings? What did you feel? We are dealing with feelings. Guilt, condemnation, and pity are feelings.

— *I felt small and worthless.*

— This is very interesting. Let us spend some time on it. I asked you, "What did you feel?" and you replied by using certain notions. This is how you define yourself: "I am worthless. I cannot handle a car. On the other hand, I am worthy. I can handle a car." This is a dual notion. However, what kind of feeling accompanies it? You are not saying anything about it. This is very common. People start to talk about their feelings. It appears they talk about feelings, but in reality, they talk mentally. They come up with certain definitions of themselves. It is not easy to understand whether they feel anything at all. If you do not talk about your experience, you do not experience it.

— *Yes. This is guilt. I condemn myself.*

— Okay. However, how clearly do you understand and discern between the definition of the mind, "I am worthless," and the state of guilt? You may not define yourself clearly, but at the same time you experience a sharp pang of guilt. You cut someone off getting on a freeway, and suddenly you feel guilty. You do not define anything. You suddenly experience a strong feeling of guilt, or you suddenly start to define yourself: "I am worthless. I cannot drive. I can't do anything."

— *If I were to cut him off effectively, I would not condemn myself.*

— *He would have turned grey, then.*

— Yes, he would have died from fear.

— *The personality constantly returns to this memory. It tries to glorify it by fantasizing and imagining stuff.*

## Feelings are not the definitions of the mind

— Personality is a mental-emotional structure. You are fixating your attention on the mental component only. I will ask all of you to pay attention to this. This is very important. You need to know yourself very well, as otherwise you will not be able to understand what is going on. So, where is the feeling component? You say, "I am worthless." This is a definition of the mind. It might be accompanied by happiness: "Oh, I am so worthless!"

— *There can be a lot of pleasure in irresponsibility.*

— This is another definition. This is self-identification, i.e. how you define yourself now. Ask yourself right after this happened,

"Who are you?" — "I am irresponsible." What do you feel at that moment?

— *I think that if I return to this situation again and again, I experience some kind of kaif there.*

— Look, you have said, "I think." You constantly talk about *thinking.* You have not spoken about *feelings* once.

— *Actually, this recurrent intellectual process reinforces my state. I feel something, then I think about it, and this thought reinforces my state. That is how it goes. It goes and goes…*

— You do not say anything about your emotions. I do not know whether you have them or not. I am directing your attention toward your emotions. What do you feel right now?

— *I feel nervous. I am stressed.*

— You are using definitions again. Okay. Get down to the body level. How do you experience these feelings in your body?

— *My hands get sweaty. My blood pressure rises. I feel shaky. I start to close up.*

— Are you feeling this right now?

— *Yes. Moreover, when I recalled this freeway story, I experienced the same state on the physical level.*

— It looks like you know your physical body much better than you know your emotional body. What can you say about your feelings and states?

Your body can shake when you are in a state of condemnation. It can shake in a state of happiness. It can shake in many other states. But you only speak of the mental and physical components. You do not say anything about the emotional component.

— *It looks like I don't know this side of me at all.*

— Yes. Your emotional center is closed.

— *I want to add something in connection with shame. As soon as I start to experience shame, I try to close up and avoid feeling it. I take a pill or a glass of beer to help me not to think about it and not to feel it. What does this mean? I should be getting some kind of pleasure out of it, but I do not. Does this mean I do not allow myself to feel guilty?*

— Exactly. The feeling of guilt is a very heavy feeling. We are taught to hide this feeling. No one wants to feel and see it in oneself or others. Actually, what I just said about seeing it in others is not true. We say to kids, "Go and apologize. Tell your teacher you are sorry." However, this frequently turns into formality. You may say that you are sorry and use the word sorry, but do you really experience the state of guilt?

— *What if I feel guilty in connection to losing my relatives?*

— Let's take a look at this situation. What is the mechanism of the development of this feeling? Guilt does not appear out of nowhere. You have lost a relative. You may feel guilty because of it, but you can also experience other states.

— *No, I felt guilty. We got into a car accident, and my whole family was killed. I felt guilty, because if I were to get behind the wheel and drive that night instead of my husband, everyone would still be alive.*

— What is the mechanism of guilt formation? Can you tell us? Why do you experience this state specifically?

— *I have moved away from it. It happened many years ago. We started talking about it, and I recalled that particular incident.*

— It's irrelevant when it happened. I am asking you about the mechanism. What is the mechanism? How does the feeling of guilt appear? People do not know how it happens. They are frequently not even aware of the fact that they experience this feeling. They want to get away from this heavy feeling and move to condemnation, for example. Yet, how does this feeling of guilt appear? This is the question. You will not be able to do anything with it until you understand how it works.

*— In my case, the feeling of guilt always comes after condemnation. I condemn someone, and I immediately feel guilty.*

— Exactly. **Guilt is a consequence of condemnation.**

*— I condemn myself for not taking my husband's seat and for not driving on that day. He was very tired when the accident happened. I saw it, and I wanted to offer to switch places with him, but I did not.*

— And I condemn myself for not doing what I could have done, right? I condemn myself and start to feel guilty. The inner courts review the case. You are both the defendant and the prosecutor at the same time. The district attorney says, "She did not get into the driver's seat, and as a result of her action, people were killed," and the verdict comes out: "She will feel guilty for it."

*— How can I get rid of this feeling of guilt?*

— Wait! I see this all the time. As soon as a human being finds out that he has guilt, he wants to get rid of it.

*— I also feel guilty when I don't behave the way people around me want me to behave. They expect me to do something out of the feeling of debt, but I do not do it. Later, I blame myself for it and feel guilty.*

## The accused, the judge, and the district attorney in you

— Exactly. There is a courtroom inside you. There is an accused, a judge, a district attorney, and a defense attorney there. Imagine this courtroom. What does the district attorney say?

*— He says, "You are guilty."*

— What am I guilty of?

*— He says, "You did that," or "You did not do what you were supposed to do."*

21

— Wait! Let us do it right. Imagine a real courtroom. Which law, in particular, did you break? This court is happening inside you all the time. How does it occur?

— *Let's take a look at the real situation. My girlfriend called me yesterday. She was at a bus station, and she saw a man who resembled my ex-husband. He was very drunk. She called me frantic. "He is falling! He cannot stand on his feet. He is dirty! He might get robbed." My first feeling was "I have to run there. I have to do something!"*

— Why did you have to something?

— *Because he is my husband, and I feel pity for him.*

— Is he really your husband?

— *He is sort of my husband. We have never formalized our divorce.*

— So, if he is a husband, you as a wife are responsible for your husband. This is a norm. What enormous role do norms play here? You do not live together, but you have not been formally divorced. All of this affects you.

— *And then immediately, another part of me pops up: "Where are you going? Why should you do that? He wants to get drunk. Let him do whatever he wants to do. This is his life. How long are you going to change his diapers? You are not Mother Theresa." I feel tremendous irritation. I get hot inside. I start to shake. The conversation continues in my head. "I have to call my son. He has to take care of his dad."*

— Take a look at the most important moment here. Why you are concerned whether some man is going to be robbed somewhere or not? You are concerned for a certain reason. What is this reason, and which particular rule are you breaking? This court appears inside you and is projected externally in connection with your breaking a certain rule, a rule you think you should obey. With which particular rule are you not in compliance with?

— *A wife should be responsible for her husband.*

— Exactly. A wife should be responsible for her husband! Without this rule, you would not feel that. Therefore, you have broken a rule. You have broken the rule that you consider valid. If you did not consider this rule valid, your breaking it would not have led you to experience this state.

— *Is that the district attorney talking?*

— So a wife should be responsible for her husband. You are a wife. You are responsible for him, and you must do something about it. However, you did not do anything.

— *So what does the defense attorney do in such a case? He starts to bring up his arguments: "You should not have done anything! You husband started a new life. Perhaps some nice woman will pick him up, and he will be happy with her for the rest of his life."*

— But he is still your husband. How can he find happiness with someone else, when he has a wife with whom he should find happiness?

— *In the end, the feeling of guilt had escalated to such a degree that it flipped into condemnation. I called my older son and told him, "If your father continues to stalk me, I am going to divorce him, and you will be left without an apartment." I felt good afterwards.*

— Who is stalking whom here? A husband? A husband who is actually not a husband? Your fantasy husband is stalking you, and you expressed your inner conflict in words that your son cannot even comprehend. He is thinking, "What did mom say? Why did she call?" Look at this nut house. Why does this happen? It happens because we do not see anything around us.

What did we start with? Why does a feeling of guilt appear? A certain rule, that you consider to be valid, was broken. No one even saw you break it, but you know that you did. Who knows better than you that you broke it? Only you know that. That is why this court—

the most difficult court here—occurs inside of you, as you are the one who always sees.

Let us take a different look at this situation. Is this the only feeling you can experience in such a situation? In the end, you have only one state in which you are fixed—guilt. Am I right? But is this the only state you can experience, or can you experience something else? Why do you experience this state and not some other state? From the usual point of view, we can easily understand what is going on. Nothing else can be experienced. However, I am asking another question now: "Can one possibly experience some other state in such a situation? If the answer is yes, then how can one get there?" This is a very important question.

— *There is also some kind of freedom there…*

— What kind of freedom?

— *I can do what I want now. I am alone.*

— So, you really wanted to get rid of him, because he (as this other part of you thinks) was constricting your freedom. With his death, your jailer has died.

— *But it was not just him. My parents also died. Are you saying my parents also constricted me?*

— Yes, your parents have also constricted you. Look, this is very difficult to acknowledge. The first thing you are going to talk about and what others will support you in is a feeling of guilt: "I could have switched places with him, but I did not. I could have gotten behind the wheel, but I did not." You cannot be straightforward about this and say, "I was sick and tired of my husband. I was sick and tired of my parents. I am happy they are gone."

— *I will never say that.*

— You cannot even think that. How would you feel if a thought like that were to pop into your head?

— *I would feel guilty.*

24

— You will feel colossal guilt.

— *But I felt very good with my husband. I was happy.*

— Okay. If you felt good with him, and he died, you feel bad. If you felt bad with him, and he died, you feel good. In order for you to feel good, you need to understand that you felt bad. Do you even allow yourself to acknowledge this notion? Do you allow yourself to imagine it? How would you feel if you were to allow yourself to experience the truth? You would feel colossal guilt. Yet, do you allow yourself to understand that you have this part, the part that wanted precisely this to happen?

— *I don't know.*

— Here you go. In this case, the only thing you are left with is to feel this guilt. That is the way our perception is attuned here.

— *The mind says, "Don't blame yourself. Don't blame yourself." Does it really mean, "Blame yourself"?*

— You come to a psychologist, pay him money, and the only thing he tells you is "Don't blame yourself" or "Increase your self-esteem." He says certain words, but he does not offer you any tools. You come to him, and he says, "You need to be a tall, blond man, and everything is going to be great. Go now!" This is contemporary psychology. He studied for ten years and now has his PhD.

— *He studied how to make a diagnosis.*

— *Let's not talk about psychologists. Look at the level of guilt you had that made you go to that psychologist.*

— *I did not go anywhere. It was a coincidence. My friend is a psychologist. She brought me to her office.*

— She came by herself. These psychologists walk the streets, and they find people. "Stop, young lady! Don't blame yourself."

— *I was on the pills for two years.*

— Of course. Pills are a great way to deal with this. I should have invested in the pharmaceutical industry.

*— I feel pain when I experience the feeling of guilt. This pain is very strong, and it prevents me from becoming aware of guilt. I run away, but it follows me everywhere—this drug addiction continues. Whether I understand it or not, this mechanism continues to work. I continue to be the factory that produces these energies of guilt and condemnation. I do not go there. Why am I guilty? I do not know. I try to do certain things, but I cannot...*

## A narcotic seesaw as a way of life

— This is a line from an old song: "When I am drunk—and I am always drunk." It is impossible to talk to me when I am drunk, and as I am always drunk, no one can ever talk to me—I will never understand anything. When a human being is always in such a state, he is unable understand anything. Moreover, he can always say, "When I am in this state, I cannot understand anything." How can you talk to him? He says, "I want to understand, but I am drunk. I was drunk yesterday, and I am drunk today. I will be drunk tomorrow too, but I want to understand." That is how this situation is maintained. People are drunk all the time, and drunk people cannot understand anything. This is their reply: "I feel bad. Go away." They progress to feeling even worse.

*— And one has to use more and more pills.*

— The pills you took represents the physical narcotic. The narcotic we discuss now is not physical. You continuously inject yourself with a non-physical narcotic. You use the physical narcotic for dessert.

*— Antidepressants affect the emotional sphere. They decrease emotional sensitivity.*

— Exactly. Antidepressants decrease your emotional sensitivity. Where does it lead? It leads you to run around in search for an increase in emotional sensitivity. Then you run back, and you lower

26

it on account of this situation. This is a seesaw. These are two sides of one drug. Look at the mechanism of the action of these so-called antidepressants. All these pills are uppers and downers. They have two sides to them. This is another side of a drug. What you create in your life in order for doctors to treat you with these pills is another, similar drug.

— *I receive hidden pleasure from the feeling of guilt. As soon as I start to blame someone, I immediately blame myself for blaming another human being, and I feel guilty. Therefore, my drug is guilt. My husband loves to condemn. His drug is condemnation. For me, it is difficult to condemn.*

— *You have just said, "I always condemn myself for condemning others," and now you say that your drug is guilt. You are using both drugs.*

— *By condemning myself for condemning someone else, I submerge into guilt again.*

— So take a look. **Condemnation and guilt are two sides of a narcotic duality. Which side of this duality you experience consciously and to which side you get attracted subconsciously depends on the make-up of your personal program.** You have observed correctly: one chooses the narcotic of condemnation, another the narcotic of guilt. They get together because they happen to be the components of a single narcotic. One cannot take this narcotic without someone who will experience guilt, while the one who experiences guilt cannot take this drug without the one who experiences condemnation.

— *When I feel that I have condemned someone, I immediately condemn myself and experience guilt.*

— These two states go hand in hand. You cannot experience guilt unless you condemn yourself. You experience guilt by condemning yourself for doing something in a way you think it should not be done. Another actor is vocalizing it, but you experience the guilt yourself. You have to condemn yourself; it is only as a result

27

of that condemnation that you will experience guilt. In a situation when someone condemns you but you do not react to it, you will not experience guilt. In that case, by saying something and condemning you, he activates condemnation in you, which speaks, perhaps using his words, and you start to experience guilt.

— *In my case, it is all mixed up. I feel and manifest both states. A man who was just telling me that I condemn, five minutes later condemns me for being a victim, insisting that a victim will always find the oppressor.*

— Yes, that's exactly what I observed while you were driving us to the train station. That is the only game I have seen you and Ed play. But do you see it? You have played this game during our trip. You have played this game all your life. Our trip was just a thin slice of your life. Imagine if you did not have this game. That is it. It is gone. This game that we call "we love each other" is gone. What are you going to do? What kind of a relationship will you have with him? What is behind this game? In reality, we see two drug addicts here.

— *Yes, two drug addicts who learned to switch roles.*

— Yes, you do it pretty fast. He condemns you, and five minutes later, you condemn him. I have seen you do it ten times this morning.

— *And we like it. We do not understand the game we play, but we like it.*

— Whether you like it or not, nothing else is available here. Do you like being born a woman? Whether you like it or not, you are going to experience this life as a woman. You will like certain experiences connected to your sex and dislike others, but you were born a woman and you will die as a woman.

— *Yes. This is the narcotic seesaw.*

# You want to get out of this drug dependency. Where will you go to?

— Take a look now and you will see that, first of all, this narcotic seesaw is in you. Secondly, this is all around, and everyone around you is dependent on these drugs. You will see that nothing else is available here. Whether you are at work or at home, riding a bus or flying a plane, this game and this court is constantly inside you. Nothing else is available here. Imagine that you got rid of it. What would you be left with?

— *Nothing.*

— Exactly. So, what are you looking for if there is nothing here except this seesaw? What will you look for if you don't understand the game you are playing? What will you call this game? You are looking for an actor for this game, but you do not say, "We are going to be married next month. We are going to condemn each other for the rest of our lives. We will give birth to children, and we will teach them to play this game too." You do not say that. No! You say, "Dear Peter, I love you…"

— *I just realized how I searched for an actor in this game. I was searching for someone emotional who would be able to initiate it. I used to initiate states all the time, and I needed someone who would be able to do it on his own. I needed help.*

— There is a daytime show called *Courtroom*. This show is scripted, and the actors play their roles really well. They show real emotions. They scream at each other and shed copious tears.

— *They are so artificial, they make me nauseous.*

— Consider this life. It is similarly artificial. Are you not nauseated yet?

— *I was quite nauseated yesterday.*

29

— You were nauseated yesterday. What is going to happen next? You are going to play the same game, and you will get nauseated again.

— *We resemble alcoholics who get themselves drunk to the point of puking, puke, and get drunk again.*

— Take a look at yourself now. You are easily discussing some abstract alcoholics, but your behavior is no different from theirs. What is your drug of choice? What do you "drink" that makes you nauseous? What does your inner pharmacy produce? I am telling you that you are a drug addict. I told you everything you need to know. Do you understand what I said? What is your reaction to my words?

— *Hopelessness.*

— *I also feel hopeless. I see how strong the fight is between my victim and my oppressor. This game is very powerful. Personality can kill itself, but it cannot stop this fight.*

— It will destroy the playground on which it plays, i.e. your physical body.

— *Yes. Moreover, when one tries to understand, become aware of, and transform this game, his personality will do anything to prevent that. It might even self-liquidate.*

— Exactly. Yet, we wonder why we get old so fast. People want to live forever, but consider how they treat these playgrounds, i.e. their bodies. Imagine a stage in a theater, where actors break everything to pieces every night. Morning comes—every single decoration has to be repaired. Evening comes—another show. Everything is broken again. How long can this playground be sustained? Both the victim and the oppressor are locked inside the body they share. What is going on there?

— *It's a constant fight. It is a slaughterhouse.*

— *How can our bodies withstand this?*

*— I look at old people in amazement. My body cannot take it anymore. How do they handle it at seventy or eighty? I ran into a demonstration of retired people yesterday. I was looking at all these screaming and yelling grandmothers, thinking, "Where do you get strength for that?"*

— That's where they get their energy. This is the fuel. Grandmothers are marching against the government. Grandmothers are marching against the wars. Grandmothers are marching against grandfathers.

*— Grandmothers are marching against everything!*

*— Yes, and grandfathers were sitting quietly in the corner, scared.*

— Do you understand that you are these grandmothers?

*— What can we do?*

— What can a poor grandma do? She can only fight against grandpa. Okay. We are stuck with the traditional Russian question, "What do we do now?" It is a dead-end.

*— I feel hopeful. We will find the exit out of this dead-end.*

— Wait a minute. Hope always dies last. You are going to die with it. We need to know exactly where to go. Most people want to exit, without thinking about where they are going to exit. You will not get anywhere unless you understand where you are now. You will just march in place. You do not have a direction. You do not have any understanding of where you are going to exit. This funny Pint talks to you about these things. Where did he exit to? Ask him.

*— We are dealing with the same thing three seminars in a row: where are we, and where do we exit to?*

— Look, we cannot figure out where you are, and moreover, where to exit to. How can I exit anywhere if I do not know where I am?

*— We can see better and better where we are.*

— Yes, but this creates a strong desire in you to exit somewhere, to squeeze out somewhere. Where is the hole? You find a hole and

31

get out. You face the same thing there, and you come back. You find another hole and you get out again. It is the same thing there. You move from one dream to the next, but it is the same dream.

# Your personality is a nut house

— Building six hundred and sixty-six is a nut house full of crazy people. Suddenly, they find out that they are crazy, and they are in the nut house. They scream, "Save yourself! Run!" and everyone starts running somewhere. They run for two hours and find themselves in front of a tall building. The sign says, "Nut house number six hundred and sixty-five." Again, they scream, "Save yourself! Run!" and start to run … "Nut house number six hundred and sixty-eight." They run and run, from one nut house to the next, and suddenly one says, "Let's transform it. Let's put another sign on it." However, changing the sign will not amount to much. All these crazy people need to transform into something that corresponds to a new sign.

Therefore, we put on a new sign: "Quantum Leap 2012" and "Unconditional Love nine hundred and ninety-nine." In this case, all our crazies have to transform into this Unconditional Love, as nothing will happen otherwise. Until they continue to run around scared, believing that circumstances are different somewhere else, they will remain in the same dream. Hence, you need to transform your own house, i.e. your body. Your nut house is your personality with its multiple tenants.

Pint invites you to transform this house to a totally different house. However, do the tenants really want to transform, or do they just want to change the sign on the building and to continue to do what they do under a different sign? Look at the history of humanity, and you will see this on the scale of countries, organizations, and families. Signs are being changed, but at their core, everything remains the same.

— *It's absurd.*

— It appears to us that communism differs from capitalism, but in essence it is the same thing—we are dealing with the same fight of the opposite inner parts. What we see outside is just a reflection. It appears to us that this reflection changes, but in reality, it remains the same. We need to start this transformation by changing our own nut house. There is no other way.

Okay. We spoke of hopelessness and of the dead-end. What else do you want to discuss?

— *You have said that inside is guilt and condemnation, and in my case, I experience the recurrent feeling of guilt.*

— Exactly. This is two times two, i.e. two squared. I see myself condemning someone, and I condemn myself for condemning him. That leads to another flood of guilt. This is a perpetual mobile machine. It works nonstop. You need to observe it. If you do not observe, it will appear to you that after we discuss things here, everything will get better. That is what most people think, and that is how they live. "We are tired of the old world. Let us have a new world. Let us call it a new world and everything is going to be great. Let us get some flowers and let us salute the new world." However, in the end, they end up back where they started.

— *I am mixed up again. When the war between dualities exacerbates in me, I experience stress and tension. I do not try to get rid of it. No, I push on the gas pedal and let it declare itself. That helps me see the duality I need to work with, the duality I do not want to see in myself. I thought that this excitation was the energy necessary for seeing. I understand now that this is not the energy. This is a drug. I get a dose, and I can relax for a while.*

33

# The cycle of life "Excitation—Relaxation"

— You have been experiencing bloating for a long time. Suddenly, you are not bloated. You feel good. You would not feel good if you had not experienced this bloating previously. The stronger the bloating, the better you feel afterwards when it stops. Am I right? We are dealing with the same concept here. You need to exacerbate this excitation to feel bad, and then to release it. You inhale. Then, you exhale. What kind of air do you inhale? Now, look at the mechanism that generates this excitation potential. It is easy to see when we discuss physiology: gases accumulate and then they are being released. What is being accumulated here?

— *Pain, we accumulate pain.*

— This is too abstract.

— *One side of me accumulates the feeling of condemnation. It grows, accumulates, and becomes very strong. When I see it, it becomes so strong that it flips me into the opposite side, where I feel some relaxation.*

— Correct.

— *It looks like I turn into this factory...*

— You don't turn into anything. You are this factory.

— *I am the factory. There is a constant fight there.*

— Take a look at the electrocardiogram of a human being. The line goes up and down, up and down. When doctors see a flat line, they scream, "We are losing him!" This is the cycle of life that all animals experience here: "Excitation—Relaxation". You inhale, and you exhale. Your heart works. It sends blood to the aorta: "Excitation—Constriction, Constriction—Relaxation". This is a regular cycle, and it is present in everything and everywhere.

So, the stronger your excitation, the stronger your relaxation is going to be. This is where you get your kaif. This is the principle of kaif generation. This is where kaif is. You get thirsty, and you do not drink for couple of hours. Then, when you drink a glass of cold water, you enjoy it greatly. It is not the same if you drink all day long. But when you have not had a chance to drink and you finally get a glass of water, you experience kaif. The cycle of condemnation and guilt is the inner roller coaster you ride, extracting kaif out of it without even being aware of it.

— *This kaif is short lived. You relax, and then it starts …*

— Its duration is as short as the duration of an orgasm. People flirt and have a prolonged foreplay just in order to have a few seconds of orgasm. That is it. They lie there spent. Was it really worth it?

However, you have this excitation. You accumulate it for a long time. Therefore, it is not about the duration of the orgasm; it is about relaxation. Otherwise, you would go crazy.

The strongest excitation occurs during birth. Death offers complete relaxation. Life is a set of excitations that allow you to relax completely. All of us are attracted to these two forces: life and death. We are afraid of death, but we want it too, because everything we experience here stresses us out.

— *While walking to seminar this morning, I experienced a very strong excitation in every one of my three centers. It seems to me that I come to you because you offer me an opportunity to experience a very strong state of condemnation or guilt, and flip to another side fast. I do not get it. I can clearly see that I am dependent on you. You produce this excitation in me.*

— That's what we are talking about. I am a very strong drug. This drug cannot be found here. I am a drug that can stress you to a very high degree. No other drug can do this, while I can relax you immediately. Look at the way I conduct my seminars. You flip from a state of enormous excitation to a state of total relaxation. I use jokes and other means to relax you. Look at the amplitude of our Process and the way your ego wants to use it. You have said it straight. You can use me as a super drug. In that case, you will develop a dependency on me. I, on the other hand, keep telling you, "Observe. Be aware. Conduct self-investigation." Until you start doing it on your own, you will be dependent on me. Later, this dependency will flip, and you will want to throw me out. I know that. I have been there. You will accuse me of taking your money. If you do that, you do not understand what I do. I show you these things very fast. That is what provides you an opportunity to become aware. Do you use this opportunity? I cannot become aware on your behalf. One cannot become aware for somebody else. It is impossible. I can create the best conditions for you to become aware, but I cannot do it for you.

— *I am not sure how to say this right, but I develop a dependency on this high frequency of "Excitation—Relaxation".*

— Yes, I understand. My frequency is very high, and I may increase it. I am a generator. I adjust my level of vibration. I can provide even higher levels, but I do not do it. I do what is necessary. At the very high levels, you start to experience both sides of duality simultaneously.

When you are in condemnation all your life or guilty all your life, you are asleep. What happens here during the seminar happens instantly. When the frequency is increased, you feel both sides at the same time. This is that Great Opportunity of entering zero that I offer. However, in order to do that, you need to understand what we do. You should not be asking, "It is hopeless! What can I do?" I show you what needs to be done, but you do not see it. How can Pint tolerate such a diapason of vibrations without going crazy? From a "sleeper" point of view, Pint demonstrates the extreme level of craziness. Nevertheless, you will not say that he is crazy. So how can he move up and down so fast?

— *It seems to me that you are simultaneously here and there, because your frequency is so high.*

36

— Exactly. I am here and there at the same time. Why? What allows me to be here and there at the same time? My personality would have gone crazy long time ago if it was only about the personality. A high frequency of vibration is demonstrated through Pint's personality when two extremely widespread sides of duality manifest themselves almost simultaneously. Pint is a life example of such a state. This is my state of being. If I were just to bring up some mental knowledge here, I would talk and talk and talk. No, I demonstrate a state of being to you. Therefore, this is real as you can see. This is possible.

— *Is this observation and the absence of fear? This fear. I constantly feel it. I am afraid to become crazy: I will jump from one side to another, back and forth, and I will go nuts. On the other hand, I observe a totally normal and balanced human being. When I see a human being who happens to be in two opposite states and who is totally calm, my fear diminishes.*

## The controlled craziness, or Extreme Way to Wholeness

— I call this way the extreme way. This is a controlled craziness or controlled folly, and the level of this craziness is very high. People are afraid to exit the borders of the mind, when I can jump from one side to another in the diapason that can be called madness. At the same time, I am not crazy. I control that. What is it that allows me to control it?

— *Is it the controller?*

— The controller here is personality. No, I am talking about that level of consciousness that allows me to control these crazy horses.

— *And what is the difference between the controller and the observer?*

— The controller controls something. Therefore, the controller should have someone to control. Actually, it is a duality. There is a controller in every human being, who controls how norms and rules are maintained. Do I observe these rules? Am I doing it correctly? The controller appears immediately: "No, this is not right!" followed by guilt and condemnation. The level of consciousness from which I speak, on the other hand, knows neither guilt nor condemnation. It accepts both sides as equal and full. There is no control there. There is power there that maintains fluctuations in a certain diapason. Let us call this power an owner.

Let us see personality as three horses tied together. That is what it is. Three horses represent three centers. There is also a controlling unit. The body is a carriage. The Ego cannot control these strong horses. Let us say, one horse started to run very fast—this is craziness. The True owner-manager can navigate these three horses irrespective of the level of their activity. This is not easy. My whole life is dedicated to transform my Ego and to get to the True Owner.

This is not Pint talking. This is being said through Pint. Who speaks to you through Pint? Is it Pint's personality talking? No. Pint's personality participates in it, as the transmission occurs through it. However, what is being transmitted is transmitted and controlled from there. Then, what is that craziness that every one of you is so afraid of?

— *Uncontrolled states.*

— Okay. What are the mechanics of these uncontrolled states? How does personality become unmanageable? Craziness appears in the personality when plus and minus start to approach each other, when you start to simultaneously feel yourself a saint and a villain, a mother, and a whore, giving birth to and killing your child at the same time. This is the key moment here. Would you not go crazy seeing yourself killing your child?

— *Saving and destroying.*

— Yes! Would you go crazy seeing yourself kissing your husband and cutting his throat at the same time? Yes, you would! You would go crazy! This is craziness, when you do something that one part of you wants to do but are afraid to admit it. That is why people go crazy. They cannot reconcile what they did with their notion of themselves. That is exactly what I show you in very small increments. I show you God and the devil at the same time. White and black. Good and evil. Everyone wants to be good. Everyone wants to be a saint. Right? If I had not done it sprinkled with a joke, you would have gone nuts long ago.

— *Would we get scared?*

— You would have gone crazy. Look at the technology I use. Are you paying attention to how I do it? We are touching on subjects that are very difficult to touch. Would I be able to discuss all of this, including sex, if I was a serious "esoteric" chap? That would be funny. However, we discuss these difficult topics. I do not get fixated on them. I touch them and move to the next topic, but can you accept things in you about which you are afraid even to think?

Let me tell you how Pint developed. At a very young age, he started to observe certain thoughts that horrified him. For example, "I love her, I want to kill her." I work with thoughts and feelings, and I did not have to kill anyone during this incarnation. Yet, we have all killed before! Look at hundreds of your previous lives during middle ages and ancient times. We have killed and raped during those incarnations. That was normal back then. We have been there. We have lived that.

— *I remember a dream in which my grandparents were killing my parents. I woke up in tears. I could not understand anything. They should love them, but they were killing them.*

— Exactly. When we love, we also kill. That is what I tell you, and that's what I show you all the time. Interestingly enough, I do not condemn it. You are not aware of this. Killing horrifies you. Those horror movies about serial killers, people are afraid of them. Why? It is one thing when you see it in the movies or on TV, but what happens when you catch these thoughts inside yourself? Do you become aware of them? You should. I am showing you how I worked with these opposite thoughts of goodness and evil inside myself. Why can I accept both sides as a fact, without condemnation? Do you accept your own evil without condemnation? What do you consider evil, and how is this evil interconnected with what you consider and call goodness? Moreover, when you do something you consider good, do you do goodness or evil? When you do something you consider evil, do you do evil or goodness? These philosophical, eternal questions cannot be solved here on the horizontal plane, but I have the keys that will help you solve them.

How can you accept yourself if you do not see yourself? Everyone around insists, "Accept yourself! Accept yourself!" What should I accept? Okay, I accept. What did I accept? Someone gave you a black eye. Okay, "I accept that." What else can you do? "I accept a disease." What else can you do? That is what you have. You have this disease. Whether you accept it or not, you have it. "I accept death." What else can you do? You are dead already. But who and what causes all these things to happen? How do you create them? Everyone screams, "We are interested in life," but I tell you, "You are equally interested in death." Everyone says, "We are interested in goodness," but I tell you, "You are equally interested in evil, as those are two sides of one equation." People are afraid of hell, and they try to go to heaven, but in reality, those are two sides of one equation. You must become neutral to both sides. Be "neutral". That is where we need to get to—neutrality. However, currently we discuss drug addiction. You are addicted, and you have experienced hopelessness. What can you get instead? You know this state, the state of drug addiction—it is a fluctuation between heaven and hell.

— *We have to become independent of the extreme states.*

— Okay. Let us say you have to become independent of the extreme states. How can you achieve that? I am a practical man. I am not interested in philosophical conversations. I am interested in practical work. You decrease your fluctuations by getting to the state where you do not feel anything. But what do I do? I increase these fluctuations in you.

— *It looks like we have to accept ...*

— What does it mean "to accept"? To accept or not to accept? To sin and to repent! God wants us to sin; otherwise, we are not going to repent. We will sin and then repent; everything is going to be great.

— *I was in a very calm state until you said that we need to see how we create this reality, how we condemn ourselves for killing someone. I was in a very quiet and balanced state, and I thought, "I am going to speak up now." As soon as I said that to myself, I experienced fear. I thought I was brave enough to say it, but I immediately ran for cover. This is a duality. It seemed to me I was in the Observer, but ...*

— You will not become the Observer until you become aware of the diapason of dualities you have not yet fully mastered. I must tell you that my entire life, which was not an easy one, was connected and continues to be connected with the increase in the diapason of dualities. I could not even talk about certain things before. I was afraid to think about them, but I kept spreading this diapason, making it wider and wider.

This is a very hard work. You must master a certain width of the diapason of dualities. People are in a grey state here. What does it mean—grey? It means that white and black are mixed together. Read the Bible. Jesus says, "Not peace, but the sword I brought to you." What is he talking about? He is talking about the discernment that needs to be done to separate white from black. That is when you stop being grey and turn into white and black. One can work with white and black. That is when you can understand and accept what is white and what is black, plus and minus, negative and positive, good and evil. Moreover, you will see the interconnectedness of them in yourself, and you will accept yourself.

To accept means to understand. You cannot accept something you do not understand. People, on the other hand, try to accept things they do not understand. That is why they cannot accept them. They can only have rituals called "acceptance". Here, on the other hand, we must see everything clearly and accept what we see. That is why I emphasize understanding. That is why I ask you all these questions from every side: left, right, and center. However, your mind gets overheated from all these questions. To answer these questions, you need to enter zones of yours that you are afraid to enter. It is not easy. I understand that. That is why I keep telling you: step by step.

I am describing the essence of the mechanics of the Process to you. I show you everything in minute details. **Our work is based on understanding, not on faith**. I transmit this understanding to you daily. You must understand everything. You cannot do it based on your belief or because you trust my authority. You need to understand why you do what you do. Without it, you will not get anywhere.

## Guilt as a total phenomenon

— *I wanted to see how I create my reality. Ten years ago, I gave birth to two boys. When I got pregnant with them, I was doubtful: should I keep this pregnancy, or should I have an abortion? So, there was this dual perception of the*

42

*situation to begin with, but then I gave birth to my twins. One was very open emotionally. The other one turned out to be very independent.*

— How is this relevant to our conversation?

— *One of the boys died. How did I create this?*

— Are you blaming yourself for your son's death?

— *I am confused. Sometimes I feel guilty, and sometimes I do not.*

— So, which state is false: the one where there is no guilt, or the one where the feeling of guilt is present?

— *There is guilt there. I blame myself for his death. I am guilty.*

— We are guilty of everything here. Do you know what we are guilty of? What is the basic guilt each one of us carries? Do you know where the root cause of every variety of guilt accumulated by us over billions of years lies?

— *Do I feel guilty because I hurt my mom during the delivery process?*

— Any other ideas? This is a good one. You caused your mom some pain during the process of childbirth, and you feel guilty for the rest of your life. Good one. Anyone else? Where does guilt come from to begin with? Why is it so sustainable here?

— *Is it because we are taught what is good and what is bad?*

— Why are we taught what is good and what is bad?

— *Our parents inculcate it in us.*

— Why do our parents inculcate it in us? Why do they explain it this way and not any other way?

— *Because personality needs to exist.*

— In that case, we will spend another billion years doing this. There is no end to it. I want to understand your explanation of this fact. Why is guilt so total and universal here?

— *Because we depend on society.*

— And on what does society depend? Why do we have a society where this guilt is being maintained and constantly cultivated?

— *In order for our personalities to turn into firewood for a global process.*

43

— Are we just firewood? We are just firewood which must be burned in order to release energy that will be used somewhere else. That is it; there is nothing else here. You are a stack of firewood!

— *Yes, there is nothing else in this form. Nothing else is available in this society.*

— Okay. Then why does Pint, who lives in this society, say what he says? Why isn't he hit by God's wrath? How can he lead such conversations in society, which is created for those types of energies?

— *A man is given a choice to begin with.*

— What kind of a choice? You were talking about hopelessness just a minute ago. Where is the choice here? I will ask again, "Is there something else here?"

— *There is an alternative to guilt and pain. You manifest it.*

— Okay. However, why only me? Why don't you manifest it?

— *When one starts to see both sides as something given, guilt and condemnation disappear.*

— The question I asked was, "Where did original sin come from?" You have answered that a man is born sinful. In that case, I will ask, "Where is this sin coming from? Why is a man born sinful?"

— *Because this reality is dual and separated.*

— Okay. Are you satisfied with this answer? If you are satisfied with the fact that this is the way this world is, it will never change. You will have what you have for another billion years.

— *That's what we came to at the end of our discussion. The situation is hopeless.*

— So there is nothing else?

— *Well, it seems like this is what you are saying …*

— I can say many things. Does it matter? Where did original sin come from? How did it form?

— *It has to do with condemnation. One side of personality condemns the other side.*

44

— Who are you?

— *We are agents. We were sent here.*

— Okay. You are agents. So, where did you get this guilt, agents? Why does your ego constantly experience guilt?

— *Because this is its fuel.*

— Why is it its fuel? Around whom does it feel guilty?

— *It feels guilty because it is not working on solving the assignment with which it came here.*

— Why isn't it solving the assignment? It does not work and does not try to solve the assignment because it pretends to be the Owner! However, it is not the Owner. It declared itself the Owner, and that is why it experiences eternal guilt. This is fiction. Ego is an imposter. An imposter who pronounced himself to be the Owner experiences guilt. So, who is the True Owner? The Supreme Aspect is the True Owner. Ego hides it. Moreover, the ego is not just your personality. We are dealing with egos of organizations, egos of nations, and the ego of humanity, which gave birth to religion, and a worldview that is based on its fictitious ownership. Guilt is the consequence of this groundless pretense. This is the sin church talks about, if we are to use church language.

Therefore, the real sin is in the negation of the True Owner by the ego imposter. How can Pint say that? He can say that because he is saying it from his True Owner. Why do you experience a state of hopelessness without even understanding the reason behind it? Ego does not want to step away from the throne. It tries to find arguments, but it cannot. In addition, it says, "That's it. Hopelessness." However, this is not hopelessness. The situation is not hopeless for someone who got to know and follows the True Owner. It is hopeless for the ego, which was exposed in using false power. The physical body is the only real estate every living human being has. So, the ego declares itself the owner of this house. What does it do there? We have already discussed that. It turns it into a nut house.

*— And it constantly tries to deny this: "This is not me! I did not do that!"*

— I would compare it to a psychiatric ward that lunatics took over. They killed every psychiatrist in the house. Today schizophrenics are in charge, tomorrow paranoiacs take over. Thursday comes, bipolars are in charge. That is what ego does.

*— How brave should one be to see all of this and not condemn it?*

— One should be jolly and cheerful. One should have fun and be aware! You look from above, "Great! Today we have schizophrenics." Can you look at your own nut house from above? I am sharing a secret with you. Where am I talking to you from? I am talking to you from There. Only from over There can you see things as they are here. Here, in this nut house, you can only fight for power. How can you laugh here if you may suddenly have a coup d'état tonight? How can you laugh when no one knows who will be in power tomorrow morning, and what are they going to do to those who held power yesterday? That is why this constant stress and fear exists.

This nut house is a drug house. Some, being under the influence, will take power. Others, being in this state, will hang everyone in sight. Everyone is under the influence here. I am describing what happens on Earth. Take a good look, and you will see that all of this is inside you. Whatever you see outside is just a reflection. I'll speed things up a bit. Otherwise, it will take you decades to see this.

Communists were in power for seventy-five years. This is a lifetime! In our Process, however, one day it is one thing, tomorrow something else. It is moving fast, so you can see better. Why do I create such an acceleration? I do it in order for you to see. People cannot see otherwise. They forget everything. Ask young kids what they know about World War 2. They will tell you Americans won it.

Some will tell you that Hitler was good. That is how distorted things get a couple of years down the road. No one remembers anything. So how can we see things here, in the Process? We need to speed things up. That is why we operate with such a high frequency. Otherwise, we will not get anywhere.

For example, a woman is crying, "I loved him, but he betrayed me! I stopped loving him. He died." What if you were to speed it up a bit: one minute—love, next minute—dead? In this case, you can see everything clearly. You can see everything from over There. There is no time There. The history of the world can be reviewed and seen instantly from a different time standpoint. Here, being in a slow time, a human being lives his life and gets involved in different situations without any real understanding of what is going on. It is only when you start to experience inner acceleration and see how the mechanisms of duality work that you start to see it inside yourself. History is rewritten every decade. We had one history during the Stalin era, and another history during Gorbachev. This is just a short period of time that we know well. That is exactly what happens inside you.

— *Exactly. Let us not talk about Stalin. Let us talk about my husband. He knocked me out emotionally five times yesterday, and he does not remember anything today. "I didn't do anything," he says.*

— He denies it. If you were to pressure him, he would say, "I was not hurting you, I was massaging you." What kind of life is it if you do not remember anything? Whatever you remember, you distort and forget. A man has everything in his life. He just needs to dig it out and take a good look at it. But you don't see anything. You don't want to see. Stalin is considered to be an enemy of the people now, and fifty years ago he was considered to be a father of the people. Can you see how fast this situation flipped to the opposite side? Now look at your own perception of your own history, and you will see the same thing. But how can you accept this if you don't see it inside yourself? Who are you? You are a fragment. I remember, "I had a cup of coffee this morning. That is it. I don't remember anything else. Oh, I remember, my husband is an idiot, and my kids are sick. I remember that. I don't remember anything else." Then, I activate you here and you start to recall yourself. What can you understand without it? What can you accept without it?

— *When I start to see things, I gets scared.*

— Exactly, you get scared and you want to forget. However, I don't allow you to forget anything. I offer you an opportunity to recall.

How much can you recall and carry? That is the way to determine what you can add to yourself. However, you will not be able to add anything if you do not remember and do not want to remember. In this case, you are left with hopelessness. There is nothing else in this case. The process of self-remembrance is very difficult. Everything is blocked. You are watching a movie, and *boom*—two years are gone. Only five fragments are left. What did you feel? What did you do? Who can restore it now?

— *We come home every night and say, "I found this pleasant today, and I found this pleasant. I found this to be unpleasant, and that was irritating." We scratch the things we did not like. We do it ourselves.*

— Exactly. A human being's memory cannot store information for more than five minutes. Only five minutes, and we manage to erase many things out of these five minutes, too.

# CHAPTER 2
# PAINFUL LIFE SITUATION AND HOW TO CHANGE THEM

❖◦❖◦ ❖◦❖◦ ❖◦❖◦ ❖◦❖◦ ❖◦❖◦ ❖◦❖◦ ❖◦❖◦ ❖◦❖◦ ❖◦❖◦ ❖◦❖◦ ❖◦❖◦ ❖◦❖◦ ❖◦

## What does it mean
## to be better than everybody else?

— What are we going to start with today?

— *Can I start? Every day I wake up afraid I am not going to live to see tomorrow. It seems to me that in order to see fear as a certain substance we happen to be in all the time, I need to see what exactly gives birth to this fear in me. I need to see it in order to separate myself from it. This fear is inside me. I understand, and I feel that. Some people cause me to experience this fear. I started to investigate who is afraid of whom here and how this fear is connected to humiliation. I concluded that there are two parts inside me: a grown-up woman and a little girl. Moreover, it is my little girl who is afraid. She is terribly afraid of this grown-up woman, i.e. of mother.*

*As a child, she was afraid of her mom. Now, when she is a mother herself, she is afraid inside. I recalled one episode. I was five years old. My parents brought me back from the kindergarten, and I, without changing my clothes, started to paint. It got messy very fast. On top of punishing me harshly, Mom forced me to wear these dirty clothes to kindergarten the next day. I was terribly afraid and ashamed to go there all dirty, but I had no choice. When I arrived there, I was chastised and shamed in front of the whole class for wearing a dirty dress. I recalled this episode yesterday. I was very scared. My punishment was humiliation. I was not physically hurt. I was not deprived of anything. I was humiliated and put to shame. I clearly recall what this girl feels: "Why? I don't understand why. What*

49

*did I do? I got paint over my dress. Is that why you do this to me?" The*
*punishment was much harsher than the misdemeanor called for. I was punished*
*by humiliation, and all my future interaction with Mom was connected to this fear*
*of being humiliated again. I was always afraid not to be up to par. The bar was*
*set very high, "You should be better than anyone else, and you should be much*
*better." I was better anyway. I was a stellar student, but it did not matter. If I*
*were to bring a bad grade home, I would be punished. I was always punished by*
*emotional condemnation.*

— To be a good student and to be better than anyone else are two different things. To be a good student presupposes some kind of criteria, to get all As, for example. However, "to be better than everybody else" is not clear at all. A child is instructed "to be better than everybody else." This is not clear at all. What does it mean? Moreover, this is what is being requested of him later on all the time. What is this child going to do? What does it mean, "To be better than everybody else"?

— *It means other kids should be worse than her.*

— Yes. In this case, other kids should be worse than her. If other kids are being condemned, while she is not, she is better than all of them. How can you be better than the best?

— *In such case, he starts to feel good when others are doing poorly.*

— Exactly. You feel great and happy when others are doing poorly, because if others are successful, they might become better than you. What do we see here? First, we see a mechanism: you receive satisfaction when others are bad. Secondly, we see a strong dependence on public opinion here. Where do criteria of good and bad come from? Who assigns them? Public opinion assigns them. Who sets up the principles of this competition? Who sets up reward and punishment? Public opinion does. Therefore, we are dealing with the game that is supported by public opinion, where one experiences satisfaction when someone is losing, which means—I am better.

— *My case is very similar. I was obligated to study better than anybody else did. To study well was not enough; I had to be better than anybody else. However, I did not feel satisfaction when someone was worse than I was. My parents were constantly reminding me, "It does not matter to us how well other kids study. It matters to us that you are the best."*

— Okay. We can see different emphasis here. Some parents compare their child to other kids, and in that case, this is significant. If there is no comparison with other kids, it is insignificant. In her case, she was put in front of the class for everyone to observe and compare her with another girl. This is a very important moment! We must pay very close attention to the context of the emotional traumas you have received, because it is through these traumas that the program gets downloaded.

— *Seeing this woman and girl simultaneously now, I understand that I am identified with this grown up, successful, and arrogant woman. That is the impression people get when they see me for the first time. However, I am always unsure of myself. I always feel this small girl inside.*

— This arrogant woman is based on a little girl who is unsure of herself. These are two sides of one phenomena. Do you understand? These are two opposite sides of one phenomena. The woman always proves to the little girl that she is better than she is. She constantly proves to this little girl that she has the opposite of what she has.

— *The girl is afraid of this woman. She is constantly afraid of not being up to par in her eyes.*

— Exactly. The girl should be bad. That is the only way for the woman to be higher than she is. Whatever this woman considers to be plus will be based on the minus. The degree of this plus or minus is being equally reinforced for both of them. They are interconnected. If one is worthless, the other one is worthy. For one to ascend one step, another one should step down a step. That is why this girl is a hostage of this woman. When one of them is praised, another one

51

gets whipped. This happens simultaneously. You need to see this consistent pattern. This is the hidden mechanism that this duality works upon. It is not easy to see this mechanism. It appears to be different, but when this woman is praised, the girl gets whipped—the mind never stops making comparisons.

— *I don't see that yet.*

— This is not easy to understand. I speak about it because I know the law on which this training ground Earth is built. I understand that, and I see it based on this understanding.

— *What can your woman praise you for?*

— Check this out right now. What is important for her? Arrogance is a very broad term. What is behind it? Behind it is a high standard. High standard of what?

— *She demonstrates her superiority over others.*

— This is not an abstract superiority. Look deeper. On what is her superiority based?

— *It is based on her* **appearance**. *Looks like your woman is using the intellectual center to put herself higher, while the girl, who manifests herself through the physical center, suffers—the higher your woman gets, the lower your girl goes.*

— Yes, this has to do with the example you brought up. Why was your girl punished? She was punished for her appearance.

— *Yes, she was punished for her appearance. Actually, she was punished for misbehavior. She was told many times that she must change her clothes coming home.*

— There are different types of misbehavior. You can be punished for picking up a dirty toy from the floor or for something else. In this particular case, it deals with your appearance. This is very important.

— *Yes, I have mentioned already that I feel very confident in terms of my appearance, but this is* **mental understanding**. *I don't feel it. I know that*

*I am beautiful in some situations and that I am not beautiful in other situations. This appraisal comes from the mind. I don't **feel** that I am attractive.*

— Do you know that you use this mental understanding as a weapon?

*— Yes. I use it only as a weapon. It is not being used to feel any emotions.*

# Promotional slogans of the personality

— Imagine a commercial that we see everywhere every day. A beautiful girl is advertising a bra. Does she experience herself as beautiful? She is beautiful, but does she experience herself as beautiful? No. she is an advertisement.

Look at yourself now. Are we dealing with a similar advertisement in your case?

*— Yes, we are dealing with the same thing here. Moreover, I just saw today that this is a strong weapon. This is a very powerful weapon and it acts with a great precision.*

— You are not even a soldier with a weapon; *you* are this weapon. You are the analog of the advertisement I describe. Who created this advertisement? Who hung it there, and what is it supposed to do? It is hanging there, and it is a weapon which a certain corporation uses to attract clients. You are a similar advertisement. How do you experience yourself? Are you even here? Are you supposed to be here? Look at your life from this angle. You are an advertisement that occupies a certain place. What is your slogan? Go ahead, invent one.

*— I will go with, "Take pity on me."*

*— Don't pity me. I can pity anyone myself.*

*— Don't approach me. I will kill you.*

*— Don't get close to me. I am not a pussycat; I am a tigress.*

*— Don't touch! You will get dirty!*

*— I can be used cheaply.*

*— I don't need a man. I am a strong woman.*

*— Lately, I have started to feel this contradiction and this constant fight that goes on inside of me. I understand that I am in the successful part. It climbs higher and higher, and she is afraid to fall down on her ass and to lose everything. For this part, that would be humiliating. I also feel resistance inside. Another part of me does not want to get up in the morning to go to work. It wants to lead a simple life that it can enjoy.*

— Describe the opposite slogan.

*— I am sitting on a sea shore with the wind blowing through my hair... The sun is shining, the weather is clear ... I feel good ...*

— This is a very happy advertisement. Your first slogan, "I will ascend a career ladder," shows a hard-faced woman who pushes everyone aside. The opposite slogan says, "I will fall down a career ladder." She falls into the abyss.

*— She is walking down a sea shore penniless, collecting empty bottles. As this woman walks through this beach, she becomes smaller and smaller. Finally, she drops down to the floor and turns into a little girl dressed in dirty clothes.*

*— I saw myself falling out of my aggression and turning into this little girl. She is under a table. She feels scared of Mom and Dad.*

— Great. This is one position of your advertisement. What about the other side? She is standing on a table, with Mom and Dad hiding underneath it. She jumps up and down on the table, while they sit there scared.

*— That's what I did to my parents when I was young.*

— Yes. That is what they deserved.

*— I, on the other hand, was brought up to behave well.*

*— My mom was ready to deliver, and Dad brought her to the hospital. A nurse accidentally gave her a sedative and left her. I got nervous inside, and I delivered myself. That is how I became independent.*

Two opposite tendencies get inculcated into a program

— Two opposite tendencies get downloaded into a program. On one side, it is to be better. On the opposite side, it is to be the worst. This is a duality. "I was instructed to be better, and I am trying" is a one-sided vision. No! You were inculcated with both.

*— I was told that I should be better, but I was also made to stand in front of the class as the one who is worse than everyone else.*

— Exactly. You can only understand what is better based on comparison. Who knows anything here? No one knows anything. You cannot even imagine the degree of *not understanding* with which this reality is pierced. Where are the flag posts? We need to have some notions to work with. Our notions of what is "better and higher" are based on the notion of "worst and lower". That is how every duality is built. The mind appraises these two opposite sides, but we are not aware of it. We want to be better, but at the same time, we are at our worst.

*— We become aware of the duality as of our state. I have felt this tendency in me for a long time.*

— Okay. Can you acknowledge that you want to become worse than you presently are?

*— I cannot do that.*

— You cannot. Of course, I cannot because I am asleep. I am the advertisement billboard. I have this slogan written here, and I am not going to step away from it. This is the essence of what I am discussing. When you manage to see this duality and to accept that you want to be the worst, or the opposite of your slogan, you will experience harmonization. But take a look at the resistance in your mind. It is craziness for the mind.

*— I have been soaking in this "better—worst" for a very long time. It was all about "duty" and "not performing one's duty". I have a feeling that this is a protest of the part that does not want to perform its duty.*

— Exactly. Take anything you want, and you will see that. Take this duality: "I want to perform my duty—I don't want to perform my duty". When you thoroughly feel both sides, you will become calm. Otherwise, only one of your sides operates. You don't even want to see another side. In that case, there is no calmness.

The subconscious director works and does what he does. From the standpoint of the conscious director, the work of another director is horror, unhappiness, and negativity.

— *It looks like quite a lot is buried in this state of fear: "duty—rejection of duty", "little girl—grown up woman", etc.*

— Of course. The difference between a human being and an animal is that an animal is only concerned with its own survival: eat, drink, and have sex as its instinct dictates. A human being, on the other hand, lives in a society and must do certain things for others. That leads to the development of norms, morality, conscience, and duty.

The key notion during the Communist era was "Party is our honor and conscience." This phrase explains the structure of the Communist society well. Why would a soldier go to war and give up his life? He must have a soldier's duty. Why would you give birth and take care of a child? Society needs to introduce the notion of maternal duty, paternal duty, duty of a citizen, etc. It must introduce these duties and punishment for not fulfilling them. That gives birth to the sphere of conscience. Why do you feel guilty? You feel guilty for not doing something that you were supposed to do. This feeling of guilt is introduced into a human being from early on. He must do certain things. Later, when and if he fails to do what he supposed to do, he will experience guilt.

— *It is funny how these inner dualities manifest themselves. Externally one strives to be better than everybody else, but internally one feels worse than everyone.*

*That's what one constantly has inside, and the mind goes crazy. "How come?*
*You are better than everyone else is. How can you be worst...?"*

# Success and failure.
# What does this mean for you?

— What if I were to tell you that you are worse than everybody
else based on your basic parameters. This statement is usually taken
as an insult here, but what is it in reality? It is a pointer toward
harmonization. Let us try that. Who do you have to be on one side?
Verbalize it. Then, accept that you have the opposite side, and define
it. Accept it consciously. Do that now.

— *I get scared just thinking of that, because I understand that if I were to*
*allow this side to manifest itself, it would destroy my whole life.*

— Don't you think it manifests itself now? What is the life you
are so afraid to destroy? What are those sufferings you constantly
brag about? This is life! You are suffering trying to climb up one more
step. What are you afraid of? Are you afraid to not make it?

— *That's the only way to survive I know.*

— Okay. Look at this life and you will see that it consists of one
suffering after another, chain of suffering that you are afraid to break.
It is horrible—you will get away from horror. This is a paradox. You
feel horrified about your horrible ending.

Why did we gather here? Did we gather to discuss something
pleasant and fun? No. Everyone suffers, and everyone is in some kind
of pain. That is what brought us together. Now, when we are offered
a way out, you scream, "What a horror to stop this horror!" That's
how it is seen from over There.

— *This little girl knows how to survive too: the dirtier her dress is, the more*
*bottles she will collect. Everyone pities her.*

*— My other side says that to experience the pity of other people is humiliation.*

— One can be humiliated by being successful, and one can be humiliated by not being successful. We have a choice here. But with a fixed program, there is no choice. It is inculcated into your program that humiliation is a negative side.

Allow yourself to accept that a promotion is humiliation for someone. This might appear funny and paradoxical to you, but this is the case.

*— For me, it is motivation to be good. I know that I am good when I am praised.*

*— How can one be humiliated by success? I don't get it.*

— Do you understand the essence of success? Let us look at it. Can you see this little girl of yours who got herself dirty as successful? She thinks that the more stain she has on her dress, the more successful she is.

*— She was also doing what she wanted to do. She was creating.*

*— Yes. It is funny. So many years have passed, but I still remember this excited state. I ran into my room and started to paint. I was completely absorbed by the creative artwork I was doing, and when I was torn away from it, for getting my dress dirty, I was shocked!*

— That's how this road was blocked for you. A child comes to know things here. Whatever parents download into their children will flourish, and whatever they block will wither. In your case, the road to painting was cut off. You were told, "This is not the road to success—look over there. That is the road to success. Go there." And you went there.

*— Moreover, such a creative expression contradicts your notion of success.*

— Take a look now at the duality and point zero. On one side, "Success". On the other side, "Not a success". Nothing will change if you exchange them: where you had "Not a success", you will have a "Success".

— *I have always been drawn to the opposite, to something I am not now. I was always drawn to the artistic, bohemian lifestyle, but when I tried to join this crowd as a young adult, I could not.*

— Of course. This road was cut off for you. Look at the animal world. If Mom cannot teach her puppies how to hunt, they don't survive. You do not have an alternative road. You cannot go this way. It was closed for you.

— *I get it now. This is the alternative to my current life. In my case, "not a success" is not to fall down into a dumpster but my attraction to another life.*

— Exactly. Why? Because your parents told you, "You either chose a career ladder or you will become a dirty, dumpster bum."

— *If you don't study well, you will become a garbage man.*

— You will not become a clean bum, but a dirty, nasty bum.

— *I frequently thought about how lucky garbage men were. They work outside all day long swiping streets, while I have to suffocate in the office.*

— Yes, this road was cut off for you. You cannot even think of that.

— *Can I add something? I just saw how this was realized in my life. I was brought up exactly the same way: you have to be a stellar student, you have to choose a career, you have to get married and have three kids, etc. Everything else was cut off for me. No contrary thought could enter my head. So, what happens to me next? First, I have lost a family. Two years after the divorce this little girl came to understand that she can live like that. She understood that she can live on her own, without a family. This is a reality. It became a reality, even though I did not even think of that. Afterwards, half-consciously and half-subconsciously, I walked away from the skyrocketing career.*

*I could not understand it back then. I just saw it now, thanks to you. At the time, I just flipped a coin: who knows, perhaps this career is not the only way. I decided to conduct an experiment and not take the career route. Every friend and*

59

*colleague of mine condemned me. Nevertheless, I just decided to see what is going to happen next.*

*I live, and I have enough money. I do not make a lot of money, but I am comfortable. This money comes from different sources. I lead a bohemian life style that I deserve. I used to think bums live like that. Lately, I found a man whose apartment is shabbier than mine. All my girlfriends go crazy, "How can you do that?"*

— And the last straw is the School of Holistic Psychology. You cannot get lower than that.

— *Yes. I don't know what happened back then. I just felt that I had to try. I wanted to try something different from what Mom painted for me when I was five years old.*

— *You transferred to the opposite side, and you are condemning the career life with husband and kids that you had before.*

— And it cannot be otherwise if you are asleep. Either you deny one side, or you deny another side. You either go one way, or you go another way, but irrespective of the way you go, you deny the opposite side.

— *Currently, you live by condemning your prior life. You are coming from the opposite side.*

— Our entire life here is seen from the opposite side. The question is what is opposite for you: success or failure?

— *Honestly speaking, I don't feel this condemnation. Why don't I feel it? I am looking for a job now. I understand that I am getting very low, and I need to go up.*

— Why are you looking for a job?

— *In this particular case, I am consciously looking for a job to experience my inner man. I have never experienced him.*

— *You are also looking for a job to make money and to elevate your status.*

— *Naturally.*

— Please, let's only talk about natural things here!

# Becoming aware of the fast transition from condemnation to guilt

— *Do you want me to tell you how I condemn you? I am currently in another half. My career situation is good. I condemn you for your laziness. I am bursting from condemnation. You don't want to be stressed. A career implies stress and responsibility.*

— *But I don't stay home. I have stress and responsibility in my life, too. I don't have it to the degree I experienced it before. Initially, I climbed up the career ladder. I did not become a garbage collector.*

— Why are you chastising this poor garbage collector? He gets up at four o'clock in the morning, by the way.

— *Dina, I am mad at you. You are so professional. You are climbing this career ladder of yours. Go ahead, do it if you don't have anything else to do. You are oppressing men there trying to make a buck. You don't need to do that. They will bring you money themselves. You should stay home and relax.*

— *Do they bring you money?*

— *They do. They pay my rent and buy me dinners.*

— *You said you were paying your rent yourself.*

— *That was early on. My man pays for everything now.*

— *She always has men pay for her...*

— *Okay, you are a mother with two kids. You have left two kids on their own ...*

— *They are old enough.*

— *Still!*

— *How long could I tolerate that? I was doing everything for them: cooking, cleaning, etc. Now they do everything themselves. The older one has finished college.*

— *And what about your husband? Do you understand how much pain you have caused him to experience? He had a heart attack. Did you want to kill him?*

— *She appears to be such a good girl!*

— Who told you she needs to be nice?

— *What's happening now?*

— We are having a seminar. We invite you to participate. What is it that you do not like?

— *I want to share something. When we started this conversation, I clearly felt condemnation. I realized I was right when Victoria started to defend herself, but as she was going through this condemnation, a feeling of guilt arose in me. I was instantly flipped from condemnation to guilt.*

— *I felt very guilty when Zoey asked her whether she wanted to kill him.*

— *It was very important for me to see this fast flip from condemnation to guilt. I have experienced both states at the same time.*

— This is what awareness is about. We are given an opportunity to instantaneously transfer from one state to another and to observe it. This is basic. How do we create this? That is another question. The most important thing is to see it.

## The bricked-up feeling of guilt

— *Will you please help me to feel guilty? The feeling of guilt is totally obstructed in my case. As I said before, my feeling of guilt was bricked up when I was twenty years old. It was so strong that I could not tolerate it. I run from it into a car accident and then into a hospital. I have been experiencing the feeling of guilt since then. It was never so dramatic, but it was always intolerable. Currently, I cannot feel it at all.*

— You are not ashamed of anything.

— *Yes. I am not ashamed of anything, and I do not feel guilty at all.*

— Let's take a look. There are two types of pain: physical and emotional. Emotional pain is connected to conscience, condemnation, and guilt. Physical pain is connected to diseases, traumas, and accidents. Both pains are the result of not understanding. When you start to understand, pain starts to diminish, and then it disappears. Yet, as we can see, we are dealing with two different types of understanding here. To understand something from the emotional point of view is different from understanding something from the physical point of view, and vice versa.

— *I feel condemnation quite well emotionally, but instead of guilt I probably feel fear.*

— In your case, guilt transforms into physical pain. That is where your back pain is coming from. Moreover, your back pain and your constant need to stoop and bend down are the result of humiliation, i.e. consequence of guilt. That is how it was transformed in your case.

— *How can I allow myself to experience it on the emotional level?*

— There is a remedy. You need to come to the seminars.

— *I know that already.*

— There is no other way. You can re-experience things during the seminars. You come here for three hours, then you are gone. That's not enough. You must go deeper. Use this opportunity. Time is getting denser and denser. We are entering a new year. We are going to experience new energies soon, and unless you understand, it is going to be very difficult.

— *I will be at the seminar. I don't know how, but I will make it there.*

— You don't need to know how. You need to know that you are going. You will see that when you verbalize your intent to be there, everything will go the way it supposed to go. It does not mean the road is going to be smooth. You will have your lessons, and these lessons are necessary. We will review these lessons during the seminar. You must apply supper effort. Without supper effort, you will not get anywhere.

— *I understand that I am running away from today's situation. I run away from work to see a doctor and to be excused from going to work for a couple of days. I will need to go back, but I am afraid. I don't know what to do. I realize that for me to experience this situation, I have to allow myself to enter it.*

— Yes. First, you need to understand. You keep repeating, "Fear! Fear!" What kind of fear is it? This fear has certain physical borders. You need to understand what exactly you are afraid of.

*— Right now, I am afraid to return to work because a situation developed there as a result of which I may experience humiliation. Humiliation is punishment for me. They can accuse me of certain things quite rightfully.*

— Okay. Do you feel guilty for creating a situation for which you may or may not be punished?

*— I don't.*

— Then what are you afraid of? Are you afraid of punishment? What kind of punishment are you afraid of? Are you afraid of your salary being cut? Are you afraid of being thrown in jail? What exactly scares you? What will you be deprived of?

*— I will be put to shame.*

— What will you be ashamed of? Which specific image are you ashamed of?

*— I am ashamed to be seen as dishonest.*

— You are afraid to be seen as a thief. Okay. You are ashamed to be seen as a thief, but you do not feel guilty for stealing.

*— I do not feel ashamed for being a thief, but I will feel ashamed if people find out about that.*

— This is a paradox. You are not ashamed of being a thief, but if others find out that you are a thief, you will be ashamed.

*— Perhaps you are ashamed for not being sly enough or for not hiding it well?*

— In that case, you are not ashamed for being a thief, but for not mastering the skill not to show it.

*— I feel humiliated, but I don't know why I feel humiliated.*

64

*— Yes. I just saw something. This is the answer to my humiliation of my coworkers.*

— Dostoevsky wrote *Crime and Punishment*. In your case, we are dealing with punishment alone. A human being experiences guilt for a crime he committed. Dostoevsky painted a picture of Raskolnikov who experiences a colossal feeling of guilt and offers himself to the police and goes to jail.

*— I am familiar with the feeling of guilt for something I committed. I experienced the feeling of guilt for cheating on my husband. Last month, I felt very guilty for sterilizing my cat. I had to spend three hours at the vet. The feeling of guilt I experienced around the animal was so strong that I could not even walk. I know this feeling very well.*

— So, take a look at what this situation points you toward. If you do not understand that, you will continue to experience similar situations without any understanding of why you are getting into them. They will continue to occur until you start to feel this. These situations allow you to feel, even though you don't understand why they are happening to you.

*— What do they allow me to feel?*

— People blame you for something. Why don't you feel guilty for it? If you don't feel guilty, then you don't understand what is going on in this situation. Their blaming you presupposes some guilt on your part, but you do not feel it.

*— I think this little girl of yours experienced a very strong feeling of condemnation toward the kindergarten kids and teachers in front of whom she was chastised. She was placed there in order to feel guilty. You were very well aware of that, but instead of guilt, you decided to feel condemnation.*

— You have not experienced guilt. Do you understand? The whole show was staged for you to experience guilt, but you did not experience it. Therefore, the situation will continue to repeat itself.

Why does it recur, and what is being requested of you? What do they want?

— *They want you to feel remorse and guilt.*

— But you reply, "No, I will not feel anything!"

— *I just recalled a situation that is very similar to this kindergarten situation. When I was in eighth grade, my school sent me to a very prestigious summer camp. Only one student from the whole class could go. I was sent there because I was the best student in my class, but when I returned, no one would talk to me.*

— Did you understand why?

— *Yes, I understood.*

— *She understood it intellectually, but she did not experience it emotionally.*

— *Yes, I understood why they didn't talk to me, but I did not feel guilty.*

— Look, both situations were created to open your emotional center. All these people were trying to help you, but you have said, "I don't have the emotional center." That was the reason these situations were created.

— *You, on the other hand, have experienced condemnation, while based on the norms inculcated into your structure when you were five years old, you were supposed to experience the feeling of guilt. Then, this girl of yours decided that something was wrong with her. You should recall these people and the way they condemned you back then. You are saying now, "I can't find the feeling of guilt there." It means you have experienced the opposite feeling. Allow yourself to feel condemnation.*

— *That's why I decided to take a sick leave. I understand that if I were to go to work, I would hammer all of them with condemnation.*

# Move to the other side of duality
# and experience guilt in front of everyone

— Take a look at how stuck you are in one side, and what they have to do to bend you in the opposite direction. They are helping you. This is the paradox. All these people are actors who help you find out that aside from condemnation there is also guilt, but you insist on one side, and that leads to conflict escalation. Once you thoroughly feel this guilt, the situation will change. Otherwise, it will only escalate. Look at what they want from you. In reality, they *are* you. What do you want from yourself? You got stuck in a state where you don't feel anything. You do not feel guilt, but you feel condemnation. Guilt is also there. Do you understand? Where condemnation is present, there is also guilt. They walk hand in hand together. You accept one side, but you reject the other side. You are constantly on the offensive side. Now, you are being offered the opposite side. I will repeat that this is what you want from yourself. They are doing everything they can, and they will put more effort into their work until you come to understand it.

— *That's why I restrain myself. I am trying to understand something that I cannot understand. I understand that I can use this familiar "condemn and attack" method again to solve this conflict, but what would happen next?*

— No, this will not solve anything, because you have come to a totally different game now; that game cannot be solved from the career point of view. You have started on the road of inner growth, and it requires an open heart. You cannot bypass guilt here.

— *It seems to me, your girl has been frightened and constricted down to a small ball. This woman of yours condemns her instead of hugging and kissing her.*

— Stop drawing these pretty pictures. In reality, her girl is very aggressive. She is barking all the time. She is not a small, scared puppy

67

who is cowering under the table. She is a big barking dog. This is the key position of capitalism. You are being barked at, and you should bark back. Who is going to over bark whom? You need to whine a bit. That's what you need to do.

— *You have said earlier that your grown up woman had overwhelmed your girl, but it looks like your girl is pushing your woman around.*

— *I don't get it. I don't understand anything!*

— Whine! Whine! You need to whine. You do not know how to whine at all.

— *Please, forgive me! Please! Please! I know I am not an angel, but I will not do it again. Please, forgive me. I will do anything you want. What do you want me to do?*

— Okay. Looks like we need to help you here. Go around the room. Bow to everyone. What kind of guilt do you feel in front of everyone here? There are many honorable men and women here. You are not worthy of them. You should feel guilty in front of us. On your knees now. Crawl. Cry and whine.

— *I will not be able to get up! I will not be able to get my back straight!*

— Don't worry. That's exactly what will help you to unbend your back.

— *I am serious. I am scared. I am afraid I will not be able to get up.*

— You are all about the physical: "I am afraid I will not be able to get up." It is okay. You can spend all night on this floor, if necessary.

— *I can't hold it anymore. I am about to blow up! My situation is opposite—I cannot condemn! I just sit quietly and accumulate condemnation inside me.*

— Perfect. We have two antipodes. Come over and have a seat here, across from her.

— *When Alina started to talk yesterday, I felt pity. Based on her age she could be my daughter.*

68

— She is turning into one because of you!

— *Yes, that is who I was. I saw myself in her. That is who I was twenty years ago.*

— And you are still stuck there.

— *I did not experience anything but condemnation and guilt in my life. My entire life, I was flipped from one side to another. I felt guilty when I was with my mom. I felt guilty when I was with my husband.*

— And now I have turned into a proud invalid.

— *That's what I tried to explain to Alina yesterday. Unless she figures out how this program was inculcated into her and how it functions, she is going to wind up like me.*

— *It's different in my case. I want to get angry, and I want to express my anger, but I don't. Later on, I feel guilty for my inability to express my anger. For example, a man does something that I do not like. He does not even know that I do not like it. I do not express my dislike. I get angry with myself, and then I feel guilty for it.*

— Alina, this is great. God is saying, "Let Alina talk." Go ahead. Scream! Let everyone here know what it is that you don't like about him or her. Start with this respectful looking lady on your right side.

— *Can I start with you? I don't feel comfortable doing it, but I will try. I don't like that you smoke. I had a headache last night after the seminar, because I am not used to people smoking around me. Zoey was talking for a long time. I thought to myself, "There are many people here. Everyone has his own problems and wants to discuss them. I want to say something too. Let me interrupt her. Let me say what I want to say!"*

— *Zoey was in bed for two weeks with back pain preparing for this seminar. Doctors could not help her. What did you do?*

— *My heart is hurting now. What I wanted to say has been accumulating since this morning, but I could not get up and say it. I can feel how it is related to my heartache. It had been accumulating for a long time, and that's how it came out—through the heartache.*

69

— Go ahead. It has not come out yet. Tell it to everyone. You have saved up a lot. Go ahead. Say it all.

— *I feel guilty now, and I want to defend myself.*

— Don't defend yourself. Tell them. Tell them that you don't feel love because of them. Tell them it is because of them that all you feel is pain. Tell them! Tell them!

— *I can't say that to people I don't even know.*

— Come on! Do it!

— *I don't understand. What can I condemn them for?*

— Condemn them for the fact that you have been born.

## Reciprocal condemnation of mother and daughter

— *Okay! Listen to me, you! Yes, you! You condemned me when this whole thing started. I know you did. It is easy to condemn me. Now I want to condemn you. Why did you say that she does not go to work because she does not want to experience stress? Why should she stress? I am experiencing a similar situation now. I am not stressed. Why should I stress? How is it your business? Why do you condemn me for that? I can condemn you the same way.*

— *Go ahead! Do it!*

— *Why do you stay home? Why don't you do anything?*

— *She is in bed all day long.*

— *I am not in bed, but I stay home.*

— *Didn't you study in school?*

— *I was actually a pretty good student.*

— *Are you the one Mom gave birth to be a mathematician?*

— *Yes.*

— *Do you understand how your mom suffers? Should I tell you about her suffering?*

70

— *Thank you. Mom told me everything about her suffering.*

— *Did she tell you about the suffering of a daughter whose mother is suffering?*

— *Did she tell me about her unborn daughter? Did she tell me that she knows who this unborn daughter of hers is to become when she grows up? Did she tell me I have no right not to correspond her expectations? I have to be the way she wants me to be. I don't even want to be born.*

— *You just wait. You will find everything when you give birth yourself.*

— *I don't want to give birth! I do not understand why I should give birth.*

— *Ah, you don't want to give birth either?! You do not want to stress at all.*

— *I really don't understand why would one gives birth with such dumb intentions. "I am bored and don't have anything to do. I am going to make myself a baby who will do what I could not do. I didn't become a ballerina. I will give birth to a baby girl, and she will get to Bolshoi. Or I was good at math, but my daughter is going to be better."*

— Sit down and listen, moms.

— *Please forgive me, daughter.*

— *I was in pain for eight hours giving birth to you.*

— *I always had plenty to say to my parents, but I was never allowed to say anything. When I was little I was always told, "Watch your mouth. You can't talk to your mother this way!" When I try to bring it up now, being a grown up, they always turn it into a joke, "Come on! That never happened. That was so long ago. You are just imagining things."*

— *Really, what's up with you? You have a great mom. You did not become a mathematician. So, what? We have never interfered with you becoming an actress!*

— *Actualy, you did!*

— *Come on, daughter. That was your perception. I was never against it. I am happy for you. Of course, it saddens me that your life was ruined, but what can we do now?*

— You want to cross everything out! Why are you barking at your mother? If you only listened to your mother!

— *I just felt what my mother feels. So, it is you who condemn me! Yes, I condemn you, but you condemn me too.*

— *I am just not aware of it, and I don't allow it to manifest itself.*

— Exactly. And because you don't allow it to manifest itself, you don't see it. You got stuck in this nice little girl.

— **And whatever you dont manifest accumulates in your heart.**

— **Not only does it accumulate in the heart, it manifests itself in actions. Look at what she manifests!**

## The mechanics of so-called love

— *I see myself in her. I've had it even harder. I was working as a model when I was seventeen. At the time, it was equivalent to working as a prostitute. Mom did not allow me to become a ballerina, so I became a model.*

— Exactly, either ballerina or a prostitute.

— *I didn't even plan to go to work. I thought working was for idiots. I was making more a day walking the catwalk than my parents were making a month. This was easy money. I did not have to stress over it. It was a very pleasant experience. The university accepted me. During the first math lecture, I realized I was in the wrong place, but I graduated even though the program was very tough. Then I threw my diploma away. I did not plan to work. I though work was for losers. I would arrive at the modeling agency around noon, spend a couple of hours there, and go to a dinner party with my pockets full of money. I was married. My husband provided us with everything we needed.*

— So, life smiled at you in the beginning, but later on …

— *Life smiled at me, but for some reason I did not perceive it that way at the time. I was feeling tremendously guilty at the time.*

— What was the reason?

— *I had a lover.*

— What's wrong with that? Why can't such a beautiful woman have a lover? Every man wants her, and you made one more man happy. Why didn't you tell your husband, "You are not the only one? Look at how beautiful I am! I am the property of the Russian Federation. I belong to the people."

— *I experienced colossal condemnation from my mom. First, she condemned me for my life style. Then, when I got married, she started a fight with my husband. I wound up between them, between a hammer and a hard plate.*

— So you have said, "You can fight on your own. I am going to go to my lover."

— *Yes, but instead of happiness, I experienced a tremendous feeling of guilt.*

— Okay. Here we go. Finally, we have found this "noble feeling" in you, the feeling you lost many years ago. Tell us more about it.

— *I was scared. I felt guilty around my husband because he did not deserve that.*

— Hold on! Hold on! What was the exact reason why you felt guilty?

— *I felt guilty because I was cheating on him.*

— Tell us more about that. What does it mean to "cheat"?

— *To cheat is to love another man.*

— Did you love him?

— *Yes.*

— What do you mean? Did you get to know love at such young age?

— *All my emotions and all my feelings were with this man.*

— What are "all" these ...?

— *Aspirations...*

— What kind of aspirations? Aspirations of your body?

— *No. That was not the main thing.*

— Then what was it? What kind of aspirations?

*— I want to say aspirations of my heart, but I know what you will say in return.*

— What does this mean, "aspirations of the heart"?

*— Aspiration of my Soul.*

— Oh! You are making an old esoteric man laugh. Please, talk about your aspirations in detail. Which part of you aspired to get there? Was it your wallet? Was it your right leg?

*— Perhaps there was something in my relationship with him that I strived for at the time, and after him …*

— Listen to me, you vague women! I cannot work like this! This is impossible! What exactly are you talking about? "I aspired! I was striving! It was love!" Go tell this somewhere else. You should talk clearly and succinctly here, so Pint will understand what attracted you to this experience. Did he live in an apartment? Where did he live? Were you attracted to his apartment?

*— It did not matter to me where I would see him.*

— Tell us about him. How did you perceive him at the time? Who was he? What kind of a human being was he?

*— He was a boy I fell in love with in High School. At the time, he expressed some interest in me. He was very attentive for a while, but then he stopped talking to me. He started to behave as if he did not know me at all. I suffered for a whole year.*

— Did you suffer for signs of his attention?

*— I suffered because I was rejected.*

— Exactly. He had rejected you.

*— I got married. A year later, I met him on the street. Two days later, he called me saying he had loved me all this time and that he did not know what happened back then. I was shocked.*

— Wait a minute. What did he say?

*— He said he loved me.*

— And you believed him?

— *I did.*

— Look. He rejected you. Why? He rejected you because he got attracted to another girl. Most likely, she rejected him, and that led him to get attracted to you.

— *I was not a very attractive girl when I was in school, but when he met me on a street …*

— You were a well-known model.

— *Something like that. I appeared to be hard to get.*

— Exactly. That's what he needed. You were hard to get, and you were married. You were a model, and you were not dependent on money. Now, let us look at the mechanics of this so-called "love".

— *He did not have to spend much time on me. I was an easy target. As soon as he called I forgot I was married. I fell into his bed the next day. I did not think about anything else. I just fell in it …*

— Okay. You fell in it. You are laying there. Why guilt? It is a nice bed. It is warm there. You did not fall into the cold dirt. You fell into the warm bed of your beloved.

— *I started to experience guilt later, around my husband.*

— Why exactly did you feel guilty? What exactly did you deprive your husband of?

— *I deprived him of sole proprietorship.*

— So, you promised him that you would belong to him and to him alone. He bought this old game, "I will serve my husband and my husband only! I will not belong to anybody else!" Women have used this game for centuries. Look. When a woman is easily attainable, it is no fun. If she belongs to her husband, another man must prove that he is stronger. This is about competition. This is about competition between men, and competition between women. He must prove that he is stronger than your husband.

— *Yes. He could not prove it using other parameters. He was much lower than my husband in terms of social status. He was not making any money…*

— He thinks, "Ah-Ha. So, what? I was able to seduce your wife, and that levels everything you were able to achieve." Look. This is a war, and you are a victim of this war. Look at what you deprived your husband of. You deprived him of sole proprietorship.

— *I hurt his pride.*

— Exactly. Let us recall what his pride was connected to. Was it connected to someone getting between your legs?

— *To something that belongs to him…*

— So you belong to him totally, tooth and nail.

— *Why didn't you think of that when you ran to this other guy? You have said that you did not even think about being married at the time.*

— Why? Because she had enough of this too: "Why do I belong to him? I am not a thing. I am not a dog tied to a doghouse. The doghouse is good, of course, but I've had enough of it."

Okay. Let us return to the question of guilt. What is guilt connected to?

— *The guilt is connected to me breaking the law.*

## Personality program that works silently

— Who created this law? Who informed you of it?

— *It could have been created by my parents, but I don't remember anyone telling me about it. They got a divorce when I was eight years old. I don't remember their married life at all. How should a wife behave toward her husband? I did not see it.*

— *You have told us that your dad cheated on your mom. He had broken the law, and your mom spend the rest of her life condemning him.*

— *You are right. That is probably it. Mom had always condemned him for his betrayal and for him leaving us. She also condemned the woman he went to. Yes. That is it; breaking the law causes one to experience guilt. I felt guilty not only around my husband.*

— Who else have you felt guilty around?

— *It manifested itself in my being ashamed to discuss my relationship with him even with my closest girlfriends. I was ashamed of him. He did not have anything. He was penniless. There was nothing in him I could have been proud of. If he were a rich businessman, I would have bragged about it, but because he was poor, I had to hide our relationship.*

— A beautiful woman should only sleep with movie stars, rich businessmen, and presidents. They would hide the fact that they are sleeping with you, but you would be proud.

— *My program works the oposite way. I had always looked for a man who had nothing in his pocket, because Mom always said that I should never be dependent on a man. "Your man should never make more money than you, daughter! Never!"*

— Great ... This is love we are talking about. "Why did you fall in love?" — "Oh, he had less money than me."

— *I was twenty years old when I met my husband. He was twenty-one. His parents were very well off, but they disinherited him because I was not from Georgia. He is penniless now. I have a little money, but he is penniless.*

— First they circumcised him, and then they castrated him. "Make sure you remember, son!" This is how funny our lessons are.

— *It is fun to recall it now, but back then it was very painful.*

— *It is not funny.*

— Of course, it is not. A sad, tragic love story.

— *I am not sure whether I should continue to discuss it. It ended tragically. A car hit me, and I wound up in a hospital...*

— Hmmm, you have punished yourself.

— *Are your current health problems connected to that accident?*

— *Yes.*

— Take a good look here. Your punishment is long-lasting. You are still carrying guilt around your husband, and you continue to punish yourself. Look at your disease from this standpoint. As you do not remember this guilt and totally removed it, you cannot understand the reasons for it. You cannot get to the real reason. The real reason is guilt. Since you blocked it, you continue to recreate it all the time.

— *But the guilt around my husband ... I am not around him anymore ... I have not been a wife to him for a long time.*

— This is irrelevant! You got stuck there. Please, understand that you got stuck there. The program was downloaded, and it continues to work. You need to beg your husband to forgive you. Do that. Beg him now!

— *How can I do that?*

— Anyway you can.

— *If I only could have done it back then. I could not. I was so afraid.*

— Do it now.

— *Do you want me to be your husband?*

— I do. Please, start. Ask me why I am so sad.

— *Where do you go all the time? I cannot understand. Why don't you stay with me? Sit down. Talk to me. Are we married or not?*

— *I want to stay away from you because I am scared. I feel guilty.*

— *Why are you scared? Why do you feel guilty?*

— *I am scared because I have slept with another man.*

— *You have slept with another man???*

— *Yes, I did. Moreover, I fell in love with him. If I were to sleep with him once, I probably would not even remember that.*

— *Hmmm, I have never cheated on you.*

— *That's why I am so ashamed. I feel so guilty now.*

— *So, you are in love with him. What about me? Do you still love me?*

— *I have never loved you.*

— *Why did you marry me then?*

— *I don't know. I liked you. You were better than others.*

— *Have you married me to use me?*

78

— *No, I honestly wanted to get married.*

— "I did not know what love was. I got married, but then love awakened."

— *I never thought that a married woman with a child can suddenly flip and start running in such a crazy way. I never imagined I would experience a feeling I would not be able to control, a feeling that breaks every law on its way.*

— *Your feelings are tearing me apart now.*

— *I know. I don't want to hurt you.*

— *What do you mean, you don't want to hurt me? You are sitting across from me and you are hurting me.*

— *Yes, and I feel guilty for that.*

— *I will not be able to trust another woman after this.*

— *I know, and I feel teribly guilty because of that.*

— *You are smilling. You are such a bitch!*

— "Women are whores. You had to learn that. We just don't know when we are going to meet our love, and until that time, we live with the men God sends us. God sent you to me."

— *It's not only me you have betrayed. You have betrayed our son too. He will not be able to trust women either.*

— *Who trusts women here? Who trusts whom here? I did not want to hurt you.*

— *You did. You did not want to, but you did.*

— *I hopped you would not find out about it, and you did not. However, I started to punish myself for it.*

— *I want you to know what I feel now. Actually, you do not feel guilty now and you do not blame yourself. You blame and condemn me. You are playing this guilty woman, but you do not feel guilty.*

— *I do play now. I have had a hard time getting back to the state I experienced back then. It was a very harsh state. I cannot even bring it to consciousness now. I can only describe it in words.*

# To get even with a husband is to get rid of guilt

— Look. You have told us that you did not want to hurt him. Look at the whole situation and tell us why you wanted to punish him.

— *Come again? I wanted to punish him?*

— Yes, you wanted to humiliate and punish him.

— *I wanted to punish him by my betrayal?*

— He really got you somehow.

— *Everything was good at the time. I had nothing to complaint about in respect to him.*

— No. This does not add up, and that is why you do not understand why you had to hurt him. It appears to you that he did not hurt you, but I am telling you that this is not the case—he did.

— *I had only one problem at the time—I did not feel anything for him.*

— Exactly. Look here. You are living with a man who you do not love. You gave birth to his child, and you have to be with him all the time. On top of that, he considers you his property.

— *And you cannot go anywhere else to experience the feelings that you want to experience.*

— Yes, you are tied up to this apartment. You are married—that is it.

— *I wanted to punish him.*

— Yes, you wanted to punish him for restricting your movements and for not allowing you to feel what was so important for you to feel. Moreover, his hold on you was very assured. If he was not so self-assured, you would not have experienced what you experienced. You did what you did. You suffer now because he is hurting. Haven't you been in pain? You had an exchange. You are even now. Do you understand? You think, "He has not done anything, and I did what I did." Well, that's what he did. He was guilty too. You are even now. You can end all of this. Until you understand that, you will always feel guilty.

— *What about the one you loved? Did you feel guilty for his sake?*

— *I did.*

— You are even with him too. Take a look. Do you see that you are even with him too?

— *I stopped seeing him when I was in the hospital. My husband insisted I return home, and I left the other guy. I returned home. We tried to patch things up, but it was very awkward. He continued to condemn me openly. The whole story came out. I have not seen my lover since the accident, and two years later he got into a very bad accident which he barely survived. He had a serious trauma.*

— Which part of his body was traumatized?

— *He got into a fight, and someone broke his head.*

— **So, you broke his head. Why did you do that?**

— Let's take a look at this situation. Two men are trying to prove their strength to you and to each other. They use you to prove their strength. You are looking at the situation from the point of view, "I love this one, and I betrayed that one." Let's take a look at this from a different point of view. They are both trying to prove their strength. One says, "You are not going to take this. This is mine!" Another one replies, "I will take it!" and he takes it.

— *And then another one knocks him down?*

— Moreover, the husband and the lover are reflections of each other—this is the inner fight. In essence, he hits himself. Every human being acts out what is inside of him. In external manifestations, it appears that someone did something, but every one of us invites actors to his show in accordance with his scenario.

*— Okay, he knocked himself down. He wanted to punish himself. But I don't understand why?*

— First of all, he took you away from your husband. He proved something to another guy, but he feels guilty for that. Look, everyone in this show leaves in a state of guilt.

*— I thought that when we parted, he felt guilty because of me. When we parted, I told him, "You have to decide. If I leave him and stay with you, you will have to provide for me and my child." He chose to run away from this responsibility.*

— So take a look at this situation. Your husband provides you with everything, while this guy can only have sex with you. He cannot make ends meet. These are the two sides. You feel secure financially with one guy, but there is no so-called love there. Another one offers plenty of love, but he cannot provide for you financially. Those are two sides of one coin. Take a look at this so-called love now. Why do you call it love? Is this really love? No, these are two sides of **what we call love in this reality**. You felt emotions with one guy, and money and security with another guy. All of this is inside of you, and one side condemns the other side and calls it a betrayal. But this is not so. Any given side you are going to move to will scream that the opposite side is a betrayer. But these two sides are inside you, the external actors just mirror your internal situation. Why do you see it as betrayal? You see it as betrayal because they are fighting. These two men are fighting. They mirror two of your inner parts. This situation will continue until this inner fight stops. You must understand and accept the importance of each of them. Only then will you be able to stop this fight. Why do you have to neglect one side when you leave it and to experience guilt? Accept both of them as two equal sides of you.

*— At that time, I constantly thought, "How can I have both of them at the same time?"*

— You cannot have both of them at this level of consciousness. Only when you start to understand what we discuss here, does it turn into possibility. But you need to come to this understanding. The opportunity exists, and that's what I am discussing here.

— *I understand very well now that there is no contradiction between a wife's duty and these feelings.*

— A wife's duty are also feelings. Try to understand, a contradiction exists between these two states. **Any contradiction is a result of the inner war that occurs inside the personality.** We are reviewing two of your inner parts. Are they ready to come to peace with each other or will they continue this fight? The continuation of this fight will reflect on your physical body and in external situations.

— *I think they are ready for peace now.*

## The work with the past

— Look. Whether they are ready or not, you need to return to that situation. You are telling us that you have a colossal feeling of guilt.

— *I had one back then.*

— It persists. You got caught in the freeze frame, and when you return there, you have what you have there. So, are you ready to transform this state with a new understanding? Emotional and physical pain is the result of not understanding. You closed yourself to these painful emotions, but your physical pain flourished. Your body is sick, and the external situation is dangerous.

— *I am ready to transform it. I can't go on like this.*

— So, return to this situation. You must re-experience this situation without guilt, with a full understanding that these two sides were created by you, and have them come to peace with each other.

Nothing will change until you do that. You are now dealing with the result of this fight. You reap what you sowed back then. Therefore, you need to return to the state you have been in when you were sowing. Only when you change the states you experienced back then will you be able to change the current situation.

— *When you say "change the states I experienced back then," do you mean I have to accept both of them?*

— Yes. But to do that, you need a new understanding. You need to understand and accept this situation. This should be your understanding. You are an adult now, and having this understanding should return you to that twenty-year-old you, and her state will change. As soon as her state changes, your situation here will change. You have all seen these movies about people going back to the past and trying to change something there. This is what working with the past is all about. We think that time machines are science fiction, but this is the work we do. This is not science fiction. This is practical work, and we must keep doing it.

— *So, what does it mean? There is no guilt?*

— There is no guilt if your worldview allows you to see that. And there is guilt if your worldview creates it. Do you understand? Everything depends on your point of view. The point of view I discuss neutralizes guilt. It transforms it. The point of view from which most people look at the world exacerbate it. Whether guilt is present or not depends on your point of view. But the program that was instilled in you gives birth and maintains this guilt. Therefore, we are discussing a program change, i.e. a perception change.

But in not having the perception I discuss, you will not be able to change that. Take a look around you. There are many psychologists and esoteric psychologists around you. You have been through some of them. Can you name one technique that helped you change this? No. Guilt is all around. We are living in it. This is a norm of life. People suffer, and no one knows that it can be changed.

— *I was driving home after the last webinar, and suddenly I got back and experienced myself as that twenty-year-old girl.*

— When we touch something very deep and important, we experience these difficult states. You must allow these states to manifest themselves. This is the way to let this energy out that was stuck in you. It is very important. It got stuck.

— *I am trying to calm myself down to finish what I have to say.*

— It's okay. Cry for as long as you need to. Let it out. Do not suppress it.

## Evolution of the Soul occurs through suffering

— *I cried and cried on my way back, seeing that young adolescent girl of mine. She wanted only one thing. She wanted to be happy. And in her understanding, happiness was equal to love.*

— This is the notion any young girl and boy has. It seems to us that we come here to experience happiness, but this is not the case. We come here to go through and complete very important lessons necessary for the growth of our Souls. The growth of the Soul occurs through suffering. So, in searching for happiness we find suffering. And we don't understand what to do with that. I am telling this straight to you. Our search for happiness eventually leads to suffering. And suffering eventually allows us to come to what we are currently discussing, but with a totally different understanding of what happened before. Yes, this is a dream. I understand this very well. And it is very painful to see this dream crumble and disappear. It is being spat upon. Everyone experiences that, because the essence of our presence here is in something else. You can get angry and say, "How come? Was I born for this?" if you think that you are here to

85

experience happiness. But in reality, you are here to pass certain lessons and to help your Soul to evolve.

For most people, this is something abstract. What Soul is Pint talking about?

When most people think of a Soul, they run to church, and they are told how many times to bow and which candle to light. This is a ritual. Do you understand why you light these candles, who you pray to, and with which purpose? "I feel guilty. I feel bad. I am in pain. God will see me, and God will forgive me" a human being says. But people don't understand who they are, why they came here, and what they do here. It is common to say at the end of one's life, "Now it's time to think of my Soul." People say that at the end of their life, right before death.

— *Yes. People start to think of the Soul when death knocks on their door.*

— *In my case, my little girl, standing on the table screaming and crying rejected Mom and Dad and said, "I will do it myself!"*

— We all have different lessons here, but these are the lessons we came here to solve. They are very important lessons for our Soul. What you have and what you are dealing with is what your Soul needs. We need to understand and see that. Whatever happens here and irrespective of how painful the dramas we go through are, the evolution of the Soul occurs through pain and suffering. That's the way universe is built.

— *My dad died when I was fourteen. Mom had to fly to his funeral, and I had an impression that I was abandoned. A state appeared: I have to do everything myself. And that's how I lived my life. I taught my kids that they have to do everything themselves. I pushed my son away from me, "Do it yourself!" And he died on his own.*

— What is the most important thing parents should provide their children? First, they should teach them how to survive. Look at the animals. If they cannot hunt, they will not make in the wild. So, what happened to you was not a mistake. This is the design of a Soul to experience this side. Look, there is Great Wisdom behind everything that happens to you and around you. When you come to understand this Wisdom, you will attain the peace that comes out of clear vision. Otherwise, you have what you have here. When people don't understand, they blame themselves and feel guilty for everything.

— *My masculine parts keep dying. It means I had rejected my dad. This is so strange. I thought I loved him more than anyone else.*

— Yes, this is how it is. This is the paradox. The one you hate the most is someone you love most dearly. But when you go through a lesson, you only experience one side of a duality. And that how it appears to you. Everything just appears to you here.

This is where the difficulty lies when you flip it a hundred eighty degrees. You suddenly see the opposite side. But in order to do that you need to get to the next level of consciousness. You cannot get there if you happen to be on this level of consciousness of the matrix of survival. It's impossible.

## See the wisdom in the situations that happen to you

— *I can't understand why I reject my dad.*

— This is your assignment. No one will solve it for you. Everyone gets his own assignment. This is what self-investigation is all about. I show you what it is based on my own example. I provide you with the tools, but no one will do it for you.

— *I don't even know my dad. How can I get to know him?*

— *What do you mean you don't know him?*

— *Mom divorced him the day I was born.*

— This is the given of your assignment. This is the "X" that you need to find. Your dad is the unknown in your assignment. But we cannot say that it is a total unknown. How did you take the fact that you were brought up without a father? What is your attitude toward your father?

— *When I was fifteen years old, I suddenly decided to see him. "Okay. Let's go," Mom said. We drove to his house. She stayed in the car, and I ran to the door on my own. I knocked on the door and waited impatiently. A woman opened the door and asked me who I was. I told her I was the daughter. He came out five minutes later and told me he had guests over and could not see me at that time. I got very upset and I left.*

— And you have been holding a grudge ever since.

— *Yes, I cried for two weeks. I coud not stop. Mom kept saying, "What a bastard! What a bastard!"*

— Make sure you see on your own that he is a bastard. In reality, this was his role in your show. Do you understand? This was a very difficult role for him to play, but he transmitted exactly what your Soul required through this role. Why? This is for you to understand. Nothing happens here without a reason. Every human being you meet, especially if he or she is your relative, plays a very important and difficult role. Those roles are necessary for you and for your Soul. You need to understand the design of your Soul and the entire show. You need to understand the script. Once you come to understand everything, you will experience gratitude. You will be grateful to your father and mother. Until you live through, experience, and understand the whole script, you will not experience gratitude. You must experience gratitude of the heart, not the gratitude of debt. You will not be able to enter God's kingdom otherwise; your parents are doors that stand in your way to God.

— *I just saw why I reject my dad. He was always mad. As soon as he would get home, there would be a scandal. I was a little child. I was scared of him.*

— You were scared. Fear. According to your script, you were introduced to fear at a young age. Why? This reality is a reality of fear. Every one of us gets introduced to it sooner or later.

— *Dad was very passive. I rejected him, and I grew up to be very active. I rejected my mother because she was physically abusive. Funny, later on I abused my kids the same way.*

— You need to see the necessity and wisdom in everything your parents and other people did to you, and then you need to see the necessity and wisdom in everything you did to your kids and other people as a result. This is necessary for you and for those you did it to. When you come to understand the meaning of everything you went through, you will experience Great Gratitude to everything that happens here.

This gratitude is the last station which leads to the first station of something new. This gratitude cannot be born out of duty. Only your understanding will lead to it. You will come to this state only when you understand what we discuss here. This is not an easy road. And as you are starting to see now, in order to walk it, you need to have a totally different worldview and conduct self-investigation. You need to investigate what is inside you. This is your Assignment. Are you working on your Assignment? What percentage of your waking hours do you spend working on it?

— *When I tried to figure out whether I should divorce my husband or not, I went to my parents. I spent the entire weekend talking to them about my childhood trying to understand what they did for me. Every conversation ended with me crying. I started to experience gratitude. I saw that everything they did to me and for me, they did with love. They considered that what they did was right. They thought that would bring me happiness. Mom described how her dad used to abuse her and grandma. When she asked her mom why she did not leave her abusive husband, she answered, "How would I survive with three of you? I was not making enough money to feed myself. He made ten times more than me. That's how we survived." That's how, and when the program was downloaded into Mom, she decided, "I will study well, and I will make it. I will be able to provide for my kids. I will never depend on anyone." And she transmitted her program to me. I understood it, and for the first time in my life, I experienced gratitude for what my parents did for me.*

— Yes. You will also have to take a look at how they downloaded this script into you and what you need it for. What exactly do you need to understand in this scenario? My scenario was constructed in such a way that I had to come to know the entire Matrix. I had to learn every axiom and every law of this world. What is your Assignment? Every script is being created for a reason, for a certain understanding. It is difficult to live while asleep. Sleep only offers explanations, illusions, and misunderstandings. The fact that you are sitting here and getting in touch with what we discuss implies that your project presupposes you getting in touch with this knowledge as a minimum.

— *Did you find out about your program "To get to know the matrix" only when you came to know it?*

— I moved slowly, step by step. I started from the darkest, most horrible abyss. I was in the total darkness. Would I be able to get out of it? I did not know. When I got in touch with awareness, I grabbed it as a drowning man grabs for a straw. That was something I could lean on. It was very raw. It came from time to time. I did not know when or how it would come. I started to develop it, and slowly but surely it provided me with an opportunity to clearly see what we are dealing with here. This was not a sudden, instant enlightenment. I had to work on it minute by minute, day by day, month after month.

— *So you started to see the laws that later on joined into a system.*

— Yes. I had to figure out who I was and where I was from. I had to learn everything about my structure here. That was the beginning of self-investigation. That's what I talk to you about daily, and that's what I urge you to do.

— *So one can see the assignment of his birth when one comes to it?*

— This is a tough question. What is my Assignment? The main Assignment we all deal with here is to survive! In order to do that, you need to have the tools your parents transmitted to you. My Assignment was different. I had to see the structure of survival itself. I had to see the structure of the Matrix. That required understanding the make-up of a human being. I have realized this Assignment, and I continue to realize it. I don't know what my next Assignment is going to be, but I know it will come. I transmit what I discovered to you. It was not easy to discover, and as we can see, it is not easy to understand what I discovered.

You need to give birth to this understanding yourself. This is not the knowledge you acquire in the usual school, where you write stuff down, memorize it, pass an exam, and forget it. No, when you become aware of something in you, it is yours. What I discuss and what you become aware of in you will be yours. But until you do that, it is not yours. You experience and feel you understand something when Pint talks, but this is Pint's understanding. What if Pint were to go away? What will you submerge into? You will submerge into the same old matrix of consciousness. It will only become yours when you give birth to it. It's hard to give birth to it. I know. I do that all the time.

— *Yes, it is very difficult to give birth to it. It's difficult to deliver it.*

— Yes, but that's how understanding occurs. I give birth to every vision of mine. I am constantly in this state: conception, pregnancy, and then delivery. Again and again. This is our Process. Every seminar is a delivery. Every seminar is different. It's a constant movement.

91

*— Does everyone have to give birth? Does each one of us have this Assignment of self-investigation?*

— If you don't deliver yourself, you will remain asleep. Do you need to be asleep, or do you need to wake up? This is for you to answer. If you are looking for the exit, this is the fastest Way.

*— It seems to me that most people don't ask this question.*

— Personality does not need that. This is the main paradox. I talk to you, personalities, about your personalities. But do your personalities want to hear what I say? No. They only want to hear things that will allow them to survive better. Moreover, pride and self-importance get turned on. I say what I say from There. What does your Soul need? Is your personality concerned with that? This is basic stuff. I keep saying what I say, and it gets reinforced. Lately, I have been speaking of Pint in the third person. I could not do that before. I was going through all these phases. I just arrived at this understanding. I speak from There, and from There I understand what needs to be done and what Pint represents here. Is that what you see if you are in your personality? So, what does your personality want?

*— My personality wants to live better and to have a nice car.*

## We work on understanding our Assignments

— Personality lives in illusion. It does not want to do what we do. I am saying that from There. But how do you perceive it here? We have just heard the story of a girl who wants happiness. This is a story about everyone here. And what does this happiness lead to? It leads to unhappiness. And what does unhappiness lead to? It leads to obstruction. And what does obstruction lead to? It leads to disease. This is something that I clearly say to you, but personality does not want to hear that. It wants to live in illusions. This will not happen to me. I am not going to be like my dad. I am not going to be like my mom. In my case, it will be better. But in the end, you will see that you are what you are trying to push away from. That's what you become. When you fight someone, you turn into your own enemy. But does the personality see this? Some "sleeping" people do not want to hear that at all. You sit here, and you listen, but what do you understand?

You start to see and understand what's going on here only when you enter and experience yourself as a Supreme Aspect. To what extent will this happen to you? I don't know. This is a manifestation of cosmic processes the scale of which is incomprehensible to our minds. This is not about some special Pint who suddenly saw something. Pint himself is a child of this Process. That's why I feel more and more like a part of the whole.

Our Process is a moving wave. We are just drops on this wave. But I feel myself like this wave, not as a drop that jumped out of it. Yes, this wave is moving. It is moving fast, and I feel myself on top of it. This wave is humanity. This wave is earth. And then we have the Solar system and the Universe. This is a Cosmic Process.

— *I bought a book about the Universe, but when I open it, I experience fear.*

— *Books. That's all you talk about. You don't allow yourself to feel. You are reading all the time: cosmology, astrology, etc. You must allow yourself to feel. That's where you should direct your energy.*

— Great. Take a look at this exchange. It shows the difficulty we are going to encounter here, since everyone's program is different. Someone wants to know how to prepare an apple strudel. Another wants to see the stars. We come from different, unique civilizations that have their own specifics. If she talks about the Universe, it is important for her. But let's take a closer look. What's important here has to do with personality. If you want to talk about the Universe, you must talk about it in the context of the reason you are here. I need a solid and practical direction, not some abstract conversation. Whatever I discuss always deals with the Assignment we must solve.

— *I was talking about my fear of the unknown.*

— *I, on the other hand, am attracted by the unknown.*

— Take a look here. I keep the conversation focused on a certain Process. Suddenly, someone throws in, "Oh, the unknown. Oh, I am scared." Another yells, "Oh, the unknown. It is attractive." This is a show. We don't need a show here. We can watch that on TV. Let's keep our focus on what we are here to discuss. That's what I must do all the time. I must redirect your attention to the Process again and again. Your mind wanders. It constantly wants to grab something and scream, "I like that!" while someone else will scream, "I don't like that!" And that scream can continue for a long time.

Why did your Soul, the energy that has very different notions in different worlds and planes, manifest itself here in this particular form of yours? Why? Why were you given this particular script of life? It did not happen for no reason. Your Soul did not send you to a Three-dimensional Reality for a stroll. Until you understand and start to realize what you came here to realize, you will not understand your Assignment.

But personality sees its Assignment as something it needs to accumulate for its own survival. Where did it get these notions from? It got it from Mom and Pop who transmitted two opposite programs of survival to it. And that already presupposes a conflict. If you were given one side only, you would not experience conflict—you would just survive using one particular side. But you are downloaded with a conflict that gives birth to pain, excitement, and everything else that we work with here. That's the way your Assignment is downloaded. What kind of a lesson is this? How do I solve it? That's what we discuss here all the time. But as the personality consciously experiences only one side, it sees the other side as an obstruction.

Everything depends on your level of Consciousness. If you are asleep, this crazy chat is the only thing you have, and you and other crazies around you create different types of accidents. But if you stay here, you need to understand what I say: "Constant efforts directed toward awareness! Constant efforts directed toward mental, emotional, and physical awareness!"

In essence, you are either solving the Assignment you came here with, or you simply accumulate experience. In both cases, incarnation has meaning. A life lived mechanically also provides a certain experience. This is also necessary. But I discuss de-identification with this experience and adding it to your Soul during this lifetime. Normally, when a human being dies, his entire life experience is reviewed like a movie There. Life screening. I do it here. I do it here and now, while I am still in this body. When a life has been reviewed There, another incarnation is created, which takes into account what has already been done. Sometimes it takes ten to twenty lives to work through certain things. Our Way is a finishing line, when during this life time, being in this body, you do what is normally done There— after the physical death. At certain moments, I de-identify with the experience and in that way, I get reborn. Self-rebirth. I create the next step. I search and investigate constantly. How many times have I died in my life? I don't know. The process is constant. I get reborn. How does this process occur? It occurs based on my de-identification with this experience. And it is going at a very high speed now.

— *Are you saying that a human has an opportunity to do it during his lifetime?*

— That's a big question. What I say to you comes from a very high Level of Consciousness—Holistic Consciousness. There are many people on this planet, and the levels of consciousness we represent are very different. We need to understand that too. But if you got here, and no one gets here without a reason, it means you have submitted a request to be here and do this type of work. Others, who don't have this request, cannot get here. As you can see, there are few people here, and our assignments are very different. People who were gathered here are representatives of different hierarchies of Souls, civilizations that have different assignments and who go through different lessons here.

— *How can I figure this out here, in this reality?*

— You will know everything in due time. Look here. In my case, this question is primary, and information that comes to me in connection with it comes in very precise portions. I understand why this is the way it is. Certain things should not be said. I will be told what I need to know. What I don't need to know, I will not be told. And I thank God for that!

— *Initially, I also tried to figure this out. I kept asking my Supreme Aspect, "Why? Why? Why?" And suddenly I had a clear thought in my mind, "You have plenty to do now. You are investigating your programs. If you come to know certain information before due time, you may not be able to handle this energy." That's it. I got it. I have to work with what I have. I don't need anything else. I was told from There that there is something I am not capable of understanding now. I accept that.*

— It's more than that. You may be able to understand something, but you may not understand it correctly. You may develop tremendous pride. That's what we work with here. Do you get this? Personality wants to be important all the time. Whatever you are told, tips you into this pride. In that case, your Assignment gets even more difficult. That's why they don't give us more than we can handle.

Sometimes, you may be given something that you are not supposed to know. Your personality gets what it wants. What does

96

this mean? Where will it lead? This will only complicate your Assignment! This is a work of the negative system. It will mislead you.

— *And how am I to discern the difference?*

— Can you even discern it? The process of discernment is connected to the work we do here. Everything I say deals with discernment.

— *It was hard for me to come to this seminar. I had to choose between English language seminar and this seminar. First, I wanted to go to the English language seminar, but then I decided to come here. I will go there in September. The system of education they use over there is built on fear. You must complete your assignment in five days. If you do not do so, you lose your spot. They do not return your money. One is always afraid not to finish on time. I understood that if I choose to go there now, I will not have time for Pint at all.*

## On what is self-investigation based?

— Take a look at what you have just said. It's not about whether you have time for Pint or not. Do you have time for self-investigation? That's what Pint stands for. I just show you how certain things manifest themselves in words. Don't say, "I don't have time for Pint." I am carrying this self-investigation. Do you have time for self-investigation? You can meet Pint, and so what? You must conduct your own self-investigation. You are a self-investigator.

— *I understood that I have not opened anything new for myself. The English language seminar is coming up, but I am at the same place. I have not learned much about my personality either. And I am totally submerged in this fear. I am afraid to drop out of the English seminar—I have bought the package already.*

— We are now talking about your fear to be kicked out of the English language seminar. In reality, every system of education and every company works on the same mechanism. Study hard or you

97

will be asked to leave. Work hard or you will be fired or demoted. Everything here is based on fear.

— *I understood that this is taking me away.*

**— The question is which energy do you use? The energy of fear is everywhere. We are dealing with a totally different energy here. But your personality is oriented on fear. It does not understand. It will look for it. You will create this fear because it provides you with the stimulus to move here. You will call your movement growth or evolution. I repeat, we are dealing with totally different energies here.**

— *I understood that my personality wants to escape into these English seminars, and I decided to set up a goal for myself to counteract it. I decided to become a great self-investigator.*

— This is great. You want to be great. You want to be greater than Pint. That's exactly what personality wants. You need to see this. Don't close your eyes to it. You need to see it. This is pride. But how will personality go further? If it does not feel anything, it will not go further. I will go this Way, but I want to be greater than Pint. Am I right? But Pint will point all these aspects to you, and you will see that you cannot be greater than Pint. You will get irritated and say, "To hell with Pint. I am great the way I am."

— *Yes, coming from the personality, this is what I will say.*

— What else do you have? It's your personality that is sitting here. You must use everything you have. Look at how I do it. I use everything. I understand that this is personality and that's what it does. But I also see what it leads to. I clearly see how it happens in your case, and in due time I will show it to you. You will experience irritation and anger, but if you don't leave, I will convert your irritation and anger into self-investigation too. I've seen many people leaving irritated and screaming, "I am greater than Pint!"

— *We are used to the fact that we are greater than others.*

— That's why you do everything you do: go to work, marry, etc. To be greater than your boss, wife, husband, etc. This is the only stimulus for the personality. That's what we work with here, but look at how difficult it is. I know everything you are going through based on my own experience with my personality. I have entered a different phase of the Process now—my personality gave up and accepted the real owner. But it took me many years to get here. I have been through many difficult situations. My personality insisted, "I am strong! I am great! I am the greatest!" It required a lot of work. I was told, "Why are you screaming? Why do you say no one understands anything? You don't want us to understand. As long as you don't part with your desire to be an exception, that's what you are going to have."

— *I would like to ask you a question, Alexander Alexandrovich. I have read on a School website about a woman who entered the Process in 2007. She said she was born again in 2009. Based on what she wrote, I understood that she was transformed.*

— Who is it?

— *Ella Ignatenko. I wanted to ask you what it means.*

— She is a poet. The word "reborn" is just a word for me. I get reborn every month. It is constant. But I cannot call it "Pint as a final version!" No. I don't know what will happen to me next. That's how I see our Process. And when someone says that he achieved everything, I smile. Perhaps you just misunderstood what she said.

— *She was talking about some special moment. She saw something in her program.*

— Okay. She saw something very important for her, and she wrote about it. This is not the end point. This is the ellipsis. What's going to happen next? We'll find out as we move along.

# CHAPTER 3
# THE METHOD OF DE-IDENTIFICATION
# WITH ILLUSIONS

•◆•◆•◆•◆•◆•◆•◆•◆•◆•◆•◆•◆•◆•◆•◆•◆•◆•◆•◆•◆•◆•◆•

## The difference between understanding your feelings and experiencing them

*— Can I start? I was lying in bed last night thinking, "Why does my personality use Holistic Psychology?" I think my personality is using this knowledge to completely suppress my emotions. I have not felt any emotions lately. I don't even see them in me. Let me review the last stressful situation. My coworker was flirting with my ex-boyfriend on the phone. I felt jealous. I started to feel bad, and then it dropped down to the physical level. I started to shake. Then I experienced constriction in my solar plexus. This excitation was very strong. It continued for a couple of days.*

— This is a prolonged orgasm.

*— I would love to think that way.*

— Who prevents you from doing that? Why do you choose tragedy? Why not experience an orgasm? You start to feel your body vibrating and you say to yourself, "Great, I feel an orgasm coming!"

*— But I feel bad! My body feels bad!*

— You have said that you feel bad, and your body feels bad. Say that you feel good, approach your coworker and say, "Listen, call him again, will you? I have a new man in my life now. Can you call him too? And please, seduce him." No?

Look, if you say that you don't feel anything, it means you are imitating.

— *Yes. Looks like I do.*

— In that case, who prevents you from imitating goodness?

— *I don't know how. It seems to me that in this situation one should experience negative sensations.*

— Let's forget the mind for a moment. In this case, you should experience an orgasm slowly moving to euphoria.

— *I don't understand. You have asked, "What was your state at the time?" I can't tell you. I can use words to explain it.*

— You cannot explain your state in words. You can create a conception in respect to the state you experienced that comes from the mind.

— *It comes from the mind.*

— Yes. You are writing a paper with the topic, "What kind of states do I have?" You don't have them. In that case, you need to invent them.

— *I want to scream at people. I want to use profanities.*

— Who do you want to scream at here?

— *I want to scream at my supervisor.*

— Let's do it. Let's find a supervisor here. Who looks like your supervisor here…

— *Why are you flirting with my man, you bitch?!*

— *What did you say? Watch your mouth or you are going to lose your job fast!*

— *I don't give a damn about this job!*

— *Great! Get out of here! I will flirt with your man anyway!*

— *Take a look at yourself! You are a fat cow!*

— *I am speechless…*

— *When was the last time you had sex?*

— *The last time? Actually, it was last Friday, when I slept with your ex.*

— *That's a lie. He would not even touch your fat ass!*

— *Well, that's not what he said. You don't know it, but he is actually into fatties.*

— *You should keep an eye on your husband too. He has slept with every girl who works here.*

— *You are fired! Get lost!*

— *Let me out. I can't do that. I am shaking …*

— Keep going! Keep going!

— *You are a small insect. I will not even pay you for the last two weeks. You can do what you want, but no one will help you. People will not even believe you.*

— *That's exactly what I see in my life. Last week, I had to go to a car repair shop. The mechanic who worked on my car was rude to me, but I could not even say anything.*

— *This is very interesting. You picked me out of twenty other men and women here. We represent different poles of a duality. I spend a lot of energy to manifest my negative emotions. I constantly feel irritated and angry. I had to go to the post office at work yesterday. I just had to drop off one letter. There was a big line in front of me. People were loaded with packages to ship. I asked a girl in front of me, who had ten packages to send, to allow me to go first. I told her I was in a hurry, but she would not let me through. I thought to myself, "You are a fat pig!" I even used the same words you just used. I let her have it. She got all sweaty and red in the face.*

— *My parents prohibited me from expressing emotions when I was young. No one expressed them in our family. It was looked down upon.*

— Here you go. But emotional states represent energy. If you don't express them, you don't have energy.

— *I even feel this lack of energy. I don't know what to do about that.*

— You might be overwhelmed by a wave of irritation and hatred, but without energy, you are calm and quiet. Someone screamed and insulted you—you don't even feel anything.

— *I am ashamed to express my feelings.*

— *I have to get into a very heavy, painful state in order to feel something. You say that you don't feel anything, but a moment will come when you cannot hold it inside. You need to really wish for this moment to come.*

— *My mind simply suppresses my feelings.*

# How to see the game of the personality from different sides?

— *I understand. At a certain moment, I started to experience these painful feelings. That was hard for me. But I intended to manifest them. I was frozen. I could not get out of this frozen state. Suddenly, I understood that the only option I had was to allow myself to manifest these feelings any way I could. I just had to let them out. When I verbalized this intention, they started to open up. It was very painful. It is still very hard and painful.*

— The box has been closed very tight. Your feelings got stuck there.

— *You helped me a lot yesterday when you said that I have to take a look at the situation from another point of view. I was able to see that there is not guilt there. I saw everything as an illusion. I saw guilt as an illusion. That's what I thought, but in reality, it was condemnation. I have a strong headache now. I saw that everyone was playing his game. Men were playing their game. Why did they even pull me into their game? They forced me to play their game. They humiliated me. Neither one of them loved me.*

— You were played as a tennis ball. One tennis player hits it, and it goes forward; another hits it, and it goes back. They keep playing.

— *Yes. That was a game. I sincerely wanted to experience those feelings. I was searching for them. I was pulled into this game, and I got what I got. I almost got killed. What for? This is ridiculous! I started to condemn both of them.*

— *But this is your show.*

103

— She has to feel another side. She feels the side of the tennis ball now. But she also must feel both rackets. Do you understand?

*— This is the recurrent game of my life. Each one of them tries to fight for me and win me, while I am expecting some feelings. I search for feelings, but I always find the same game. And I feel guilty again. Yesterday, I saw that this so-called love is an illusion.*

— Take a look at this. The tennis ball analogy is very good. Tennis player A hits it and it flies toward tennis player B. The ball is hurting. It is screaming, "You are a nasty son of a bitch! Bastard!" It has just been hit. But as it flies toward tennis player B, it starts to smile, "That's where my love is!" That's what this ball experiences on the way. It approaches tennis player B, and gets hit on the nose. Crying, it flies back, "You are a nasty son of a bitch!" The time span that this flight takes depends on the intensity of the game.

*— I just saw a couple of other situations from my life. Love is an illusion. It does not exist here. But a woman searches for these feelings. She knows they exist on a certain level, and she searches for them. But she searches in the wrong place. She searches for them amongst men who play different games.*

— But you can say the same thing about men. They will tell you that they search for them amongst women who play different games.

*— I feel tremendous hatred toward every man I have been with for using me in their games and for fooling me.*

— What does the "state of hatred" represent?

*— The state of hatred? It appeared to me that I loved each one of them, and I thought they both loved me. But I just saw that there was no love there. Each one of them had his own interest in mind. One man wanted to snatch me from the more successful guy as a prize in order to elevate himself in his own eyes. Another one used my openness and naivety to assert himself, thinking that he was being loved not for his status and money, but for his own sake.*

— That's good. But let's take a closer look. What about you? Are you really such a nice and clean tennis ball? You supported both of

104

them in their game. Now you are saying, "I just saw it." But that's what you thought back then too. It's not just them who were playing you, you've played them too.

— *Yes, I did. And now I can see that I was playing a very serious game.*

— Yes, and they played too.

— *Yes, they did.*

— So, what kind of a game did you play, and what can we get out of it? No experience here is meaningless. Do you understand that? You thought you played the game called "love", but you have actually played a different game.

**You must use the right word to name this game, and you have to figure out what kind of experience you acquired while playing this game. Otherwise, this game will continue to recur. You will continue to replay and experience the same experience until you understand and de-identify with it. To de-identify with a certain experience means to see it. To see it means to describe it and to extract everything you need from it. If that does not happen, it will continue to recur.**

— *It seems to me that this was the way to close my feelings.*

— No, nothing was closed. Quite the opposite…

— *I felt passion, and then I felt guilt.*

— You did not close them. You have opened certain feelings, but it turned out these were not the feelings you wanted. But those were feelings.

— *Yes, I have experienced very strong emotional states. I did not want to experience them, but I did. Perhaps they have prompted me to start searching for something new. In experiencing these difficult states, I started to think about something else. Perhaps I am here as a result of this game. I was trying to find the exit, and I wound up here.*

# The makeup of the world of illusions

— As we enter this world, we are assigned a certain program. We strive for something good and noble. But in reality, this world is illusory. Every one of you has encountered this word before, and intellectually some of you accept that. But if I were to hit you with a stick, you would experience pain. If I were to rob you of your money or take your man away, you would experience pain. Then what kind of a relationship do you have with these illusions? In this case, you are an illusion amongst the illusions. So, what's going on here? Why are we here? We are the illusion in the world of illusions, and we move in illusory notions. What are we learning? Tell me.

— *We are passing our lessons.*

— What kind of lessons? What is the meaning of these lessons? What does it mean to learn and pass the lesson?

— *We accumulate these illusory feelings and experiences. Based on them, we will strive toward other real feelings and experiences.*

— Yes, this is true in the end, and not many get there. We are offered a set of illusions here. Everyone is offered a set. But these illusions are not called illusions. They are called, "the meaning of life," and people scream, yell, and insult each other for them. They do not perceive these illusions as illusions.

So, what is the meaning of these lessons?

Let's take a look at the temptation of Christ. The Devil was tempting him. But look at any other human being and you will see that he is experiencing the same temptations. The forms of these temptations may differ slightly, but in essence, every one of us experiences similar temptations. The Devil told him, "Be the king of this world," but Jesus said, "I will not be the king, because I don't want to lose myself."

What does each man and woman go through here? We all go through temptation by illusions. A "sleeping" human being is such an illusion. And he is tempted by it, because he is it. When you understand that you are a personage, that you are in the illusion and outside of it, you start to experience these illusions differently. How?

— *We start to investigate ourselves through these illusions.*

— What does it mean "to investigate ourselves"? In reality, you are investigating the illusions, because nothing else is offered here. Who investigates them and with what aim?

— *Personality is illusory. We investigate our personalities.*

— Who are these *we*? Okay. What does Pint do? Let's look at Pint. He is submerged in the world of illusions himself, and he is another illusion himself.

— *He does not submerge fully?*

— Is that so?

— *Okay. You submerge in it, but you see it as an illusion.*

— And how does Pint come to see an illusion as an illusion? What kind of lessons does he go through? How does he go through them? What is the essence of these lessons? How does he meet them? How does he get submerged into them? How does he get out of them?

— *First of all, he sees the fight and the resistance of the dualities in every situation. He does not run away from fear and pain the way we do but allows himself to experience both sides of the duality. Then he connects them. This energy allows him to rise above the same or similar situation the next time.*

— Good. So, Pint knows the mechanisms that these illusions work on. He does not just say, "Everything here is an illusion," as many people say. No, he received a certain knowledge, and he discovered how this world is made. This entire world is an illusion which was created a certain way. When Pint was young, he used to look at the world and think, "How is this possible? People are crazy.

Why do we see what we see? Why do trains run their course and cars drive on the roads? Why do buildings get build? Why do corporations continue to work? Things work, but when you observe individual people, you see that they are all crazy. How is it possible to accomplish something in a state of total chaos? How can people, who say one thing in the morning and forget what they have said in the afternoon, follow something and get somewhere?" Those were the questions Pint asked.

Then he started to look at what moves a human being, and he saw that it was a program. The mind comes up with explanations, but these explanations have nothing to do with reality. A man says, "I love" and does something completely opposite to what he says. What can we do with it? Take a look at the notion which is common here: "I want something, and I receive it." But I see that a human being says that he wants it, but does something totally opposite to what he says. In this case, where does this opposite come from? Why does he, while insisting on one thing, do something completely opposite? Those were my questions. And they brought me to investigate the program. I saw that it was paradoxical. I saw that every program has two directors, and each one of them is shooting his own movie. The only thing the mind does, it comes up with explanations.

A human being is constantly in a hallucinogenic state. Certain things appear in his head that have nothing to do with reality, they are just explanations. He can use different explanations to explain what he does, and it seems to him that this is what he does. It turns out, he has no idea why he does what he does, and yet he does it. So, how can we explain why he does what he does?

Let's imagine you got a watch that could talk. You ask this watch, "Why do you move your hands all the time?" What kind of explanations could you get? You could hear back, "I am bored. This is the way I entertain myself."

— "*I don't know anything else. This is my work.*"

— "This is my work, and I am getting paid for it. This is my way to contribute to cosmic evolution" — that's what an esoteric watch will say. A regular watch would say, "When I get to where I am going to, I will get a present."

But all these watches do the same thing. They move. They all move with the same speed. Each one of them has its own explanation, and these explanations are very different.

A man wanted to understand why the watch handles move, and he started to talk to them. He received several different explanations, and now he is confused. He should have investigated the mechanisms that operate these watches, because that's what moves the hands. That's what I started to do. I started to investigate the mechanism of this watch through myself, because I am one of these mechanisms. It took me years to get to know myself, but I finally did it. However, in the process of investigation, I changed. I turn into someone who investigates more than the watch that ticks.

This has to do with our conversation about how Pint started to see what happens the way it happens. Not how people explain these events—they don't see this—but how these events really happen. Let's return to our watch analogy. A watch sees that its hands move with a certain speed. A watch gives a certain explanation as to why this is the case. But this watch does not see its own mechanism that moves its own hands. Now, we are back to the question with which we started. What does Pint encounter all the time in this world? What kind of a world is it? This is the world of illusions, and he is also an illusion. So, what is Pint being offered? Pint is being offered different types of illusions. But how are they being offered to him? No one comes to him asking him to become the king of the world. No, this is not the case. He is offered these illusions on a daily basis in the course of daily events. Let's take Zoey, for example. What was she offered? What did she go through when she was young? She went through a certain illusion.

*— And she perceives this illusion differently now. This illusion changes like a kaleidoscope, depending on the point of view.*

## To see illusion as illusion

— Yes, but why did Zoey receive an opportunity to see illusion as an illusion? Let's say Zoey did not meet Pint. What would have happened? In that case, this illusion would not be seen as an illusion by her. A certain mechanism would continue to work and create the same illusion in the context of the external world. She would continue to be pulled into it and replay the same thing again and again. So, what exactly happened to Zoey, which resulted in her starting to see this illusion as an illusion?

*— She was able to see it not out of personality, but from the point of observation that sees the entire picture.*

— Exactly. And from that point we can see this picture the way it really is, i.e. as a mechanism. So, why was Zoey not able to see it the way it is back then, and why can she see it differently now?

*— Because she was totally identified with her role back then.*

— Yes. She was totally identified with her role back then, and she had certain explanations for what was happening. She had certain explanations, but she did not see the mechanisms. That's what I discuss all the time. **Explanations are the result of illusions. Illusion gives birth to explanations, and through these explanations it maintains and prolongs itself.** It does not change itself.

*— It does not change itself. On top of experiencing this illusion, lately I have started to experience a physical disease. This illusion gets stronger.*

— I call this process crystallization. This illusion, and you going through it, creates an inner crystallization of thoughts, feelings, and physical sensations. This is something that is being manifested in you. This is similar to a child who is like a clean piece of paper being drawn on. When you take his history, you see a collection of paintings. When this child grows up, he identifies with all of these paintings. He starts to manifest and express the paintings that were drawn in him. This is what I call crystallization. And he uses explanations that were born at the time these paintings appeared. In this way, he becomes an illusion that is already embodied, and he considers himself to be that illusion.

So, look at Pint's process. Pint goes through an illusion. He enters it and experiences it like any other human being on this planet. But then he gets out of it and sees it as an illusion. How does he get out of this illusion?

— *He has to see it.*

— This is a mandatory condition, but to see it is not enough.

— *He has to experience it.*

— He has to experience it. That's true. But what does he have to do next? The term Pint uses is de-identification. Pint has lived through all these things, and he continues to live through them, but then he de-identifies with them.

What does it mean to de-identify? He understands that what he just lived through is an illusion. He has accumulated the experience of living through this illusion, but he detaches himself from it.

Next. What does he talk to you about all the time? He talks about the mechanism of illusions. Why does he use the word "mechanism" all the time? Why does he tell you what love is?

Why does he explain the mechanisms of the appearance of guilt and condemnation? What does he ask you all the time? He asks you, "How does it work? What is the mechanism of it?" The common mechanism is a program. But every program consists of small sub-programs, each one of which has its own mechanics. That's what Pint is interested in when he talks to you. But that is what he does himself in relationship to himself.

How does he know all these mechanisms? He knows all these mechanisms because he experiences all of this, and then he gets out of this experience by de-identifying with it, i.e. by seeing a mechanism.

— *So, it is not enough to experience something, one has to review it later on.*

— Correct. What is the difference between me and other people who call themselves enlightened? The average material man wants to get into a position of power and to become a CEO or CFO of a major corporation. The spiritual man wants to become enlightened. What does it mean to become "enlightened"? What is the difference between Pint and other enlightened human beings?

— *They get enlightened suddenly and instantly.*

— Do they understand what happened to them? Do they see the mechanisms of these experiences? This is a question. Someone gets enlightened, and he is sitting on a street corner with a happy smile on his face, saying to people who pass him by, "Be happy! Love each other!" Does the state he is in differ from the state of the people to whom he is speaking? It is possible. But what can he say about his Way? What can he say about states and experiences he has been in and experienced before and his current states and experiences? Yes, he walked a certain path and he talks about it to other people, but in trying to do what he did, these people don't get anywhere. But he got what he got. Why did he get it? Why can't other people get it?

What does Pint do? He clearly shows every mechanism he has investigated on his way through these illusions, and then he says, "Take a good look! Your mechanisms are the same." Pint is not unique. This is the principle upon which this reality is built. You start to investigate, and you confirm that this is the case based on your own experience.

## Why does a Soul need to experience Separation?

*— I would like to ask you a question. Our Soul knows what Wholeness is and what Separation is pretty well. Why does it need to experience Separation?*

— There are many ways to answer this question. We are dealing with different Souls here. There are very young Souls here that don't know anything about Wholeness. The fact that Pint talks about his Supreme Aspect and about the fact that he serves the Highest Consciousness and happens to be this Holistic Consciousness is quite an exclusive vision. It does not apply to every Soul. Every Soul at a given stage of development has a certain ceiling. Is it at the Holistic level? That's a big question. Do you even understand what Wholeness is? This is the context in which every Soul must pass its lessons. This is something most people fail to get in touch with during their incarnation on earth. This something will be open after death and to the point that is necessary.

Why does a Soul enter this world? This is another multidimensional question. I can offer you one answer. God's House has many floors. It's a finite number, but there are many of them. We are on the lowest floor. But this is God's House, nevertheless, and it has to be mastered and made habitable. That's what we do.

113

Let's look at the level of consciousness intrinsic to this physical world. What happens when people discover a big deposit of coal somewhere? What happens next? People dig channels and miners descend there to bring this coal to the surface. Recall how it was done during the nineteenth century. People did not have sophisticated machinery to help them do that. They would go there with chisels and hammers. Was it hard? Yes, it was hard. Was it necessary? Yes, it was necessary. So, some people went there and did this necessary work. Similar to these miners, we extract something very important in this basement of the universe. Imagine that one of these miners were to put his hammer down because a thought popped into his head: "Why am I here? Why are we here? Why are we digging here?" Other miners come to him, drop their hammers, sit down in circle around him, and start to speculate on these questions. They are here! They need to do what they need to do! We are here in a similar fashion. So, what are we going to do? Are we going to philosophize, "Why are we here?" or do what we need to do? So, what do we need to do? We need to learn to see illusions as illusions. We need to pass through all the illusions, see them as illusions, and see their mechanisms. **That will allow us to become neutral**.

— *To put it differently, we need to accumulate a certain experience and to become aware of it.*

— Correct. Experience is energy. As these miners extract coal, we extract the necessary experience. We extract the experience, which happens to be energy, by living through it. Do you understand? That's what it is. We extract this energy by experiencing our earthly lessons.

Look at these two scenarios. You take a math textbook. You find a certain assignment, read it, accept the conditions of this assignment, and start to solve it. Another option. You suddenly get into this assignment, it becomes alive, and you live through it. You experience

114

the train that runs from point "A" to point "B". You experience the distance it travels, and everything connected to it. This is the live assignment. It gets born in you, and you become the live assignment.

Take a look at this. These dreams that you see at night. It appears to you that you are a certain personage in these dreams. These dreams are set up in a certain context, and they are full of actions. Are you this personage or the entire dream? Someone attacks you. Are you the attacker or the one who is being attacked? Are you both of them? What we are presently submerged into is also a dream. So, who are you, Zoey? Are you those guys who fooled you? Are you a poor, little girl who was fooled by those bad guys? You are in a woman's body. This is a role you play. So, who am I? I am the assignment, and these are the conditions of this assignment. I am the conditions of this assignment. Until I come to understand these conditions, I will not understand, and I will not solve this assignment. The paradox is that each one of us represents a set of such assignments. But, at the same time, being an alive condition in this set of assignments, we somehow cannot understand the assignment itself. We keep looking at it from one point of view only, even if we agree that this is an assignment. Imagine, you are trying to solve a puzzle with five unknowns, but you see yourself as one unknown only. Can you understand the entire puzzle in this case? You can only solve it if you know all the conditions.

— *I don't get it. Why are we dealing with this, when eighty percent of people do not even want to know about these assignments? We were sent here to solve these assignments, but everything here is made in such a way that we get further and further away from solving them. Most of us live through life without any understanding of it.*

— Yes. This is exclusive knowledge.

— *Have I gotten it right? Would we be more useful for those who sent us if we were to solve these assignments?*

115

— No. In order to come to understand what I discuss, one has to live through many lives. One must be on such a level of consciousness and in such a state, where one would be able to see this. This assignment is being solved over centuries. But the early part of the solution occurs through the accumulation of experience, pure accumulation without any understanding of it.

— *So, these eighty percent who don't want to work on solving their assignments are young Souls who accumulate the required experience? Do I understand this correctly?*

— First of all, it is not eighty but ninety nine percent. What we are dealing with here is very exclusive.

— *But other schools arrive at the same thing in the end. Perhaps they use different routes and do not move as fast as we do, but …*

— Okay. There are many creatures in this world. Take cats, for example. Why are they here?

— *They are here for love.*

— Yes, that's what Svetlana thinks. But ask a cat why it's here. Ask an ant why he is here. What will they say? They will not answer you. But you may have your own explanations. These are your notions, and quite likely they are very different from the real reasons they are here. Ask a fish. Ask a tree. Talk to them. Now look at people. Seven billion of them are here. What are their aims? Why are they here? They have different aims, similarly to the cats that are here with us. But how does a cat perceive you? And how do you perceive a cat?

How does a man perceive other people? What is the assignment he came here with? Who sent him and with what was he sent? Few people are interested in what I discuss. We see that. What are they interested in? They are interested in something else, and they do what they are interested in. Some people fight and kill people. Other people plow the earth and give birth to people. What do they learn in the process? They learn many different things. The difference between people sometimes is as big as between a man and an ant, even though both belong to the same group, and both carry a passport. There is a great difference between people. Someone is closer to an animal, while another is closer to a star. Do you understand? This is our diapason.

— *Personality immediately transfers it into pride.*

— That's the reason you are not given this information. Not everything was given to me at once, and not everything is given to me, because ego will try to transform everything into pride. **You must become neutral.** That's when you will be given what you can take. If you are given it ahead of time, you will choke on your own pride and you will submerge into the deep "sleep".

Let's return to what we've discussed. This is a playground where we go through the experience of multiple illusions. We will only be able to get out of here when we see all the illusions as illusions. But my Way will require you not only to see these illusions as illusions, but also to understand the entire working mechanism of these illusions. My task was and continues to be seeing the Matrix of Thought that controls this world. It is primary. It has been said that in the beginning there was a word.

— *They say that the correct translation is, "In the beginning there was a structure."*

— Yes, the structure of the thought process.

# The structure of the thought process, the essence of which is separation and war

— *Whose thought process was it?*

— Good question. Let's take a look. A certain structure of thought is born. Let's use some concrete examples to understand it better. There is a computer and a certain environment called Windows. It might be a different environment, but let's take Windows. A number of programs are created there. Those are different programs, but they are all supported by Windows. If you don't have Windows, these programs will not be able work. This Windows is a structure of thought process, and it gives birth to and supports many sub-programs. **The essence of all these programs and subprograms is separation and war. This is the program of separation and war, i.e. the program of survival.** This structure or this environment does not support a new idea. It has not been downloaded into it.

— *But we do occasionally have thoughts that there is something beyond survival, because survival does not offer what a human being calls happiness.*

— "There is something beyond survival." This is a great thought that gives birth to the notion of God. And what happens next? This thought leads to people praying to God, praying for survival again. Everything that appears in this environment is connected to survival. Everything here starts and ends with survival.

— *Why do these thoughts come to us then?*

— Who is asking the question? The one who the thoughts come from or the one who they come to?

— *If we are to talk about the rules of the game of this world, everything here is geared toward survival. And if we are given these thoughts with these rules of the game, it means it is necessary for some reason. Am I right?*

— This is a question for you to answer. Work on it. I have the answers to this question, and I spoke about it quite a few times. You could have had some notions about it, but you don't. **And this is the law here. The answer will come only when you ask the question.**

You will not hear what Pint says unless this question is dramatized in you. Everyone matures for his question here in due time.

**I repeat, "Keep listening to these recordings again and again," because what we have discussed during earlier seminars will answer many of your questions. You did not hear these answers because at the time you did not have a question corresponding to this answer.** The basic part of our work is to generate a question in you. You will see it yourself. I have said what I have just said many times before, but the question appeared in you only now. And if it remains in you, you will try to figure out something in connection with this question. There are key illusions in this world of illusions. Those are the illusions that are considered to be the most real here. I would ask you to name the key illusions you consider to be real. I called them illusions, but they are probably not illusions for you.

— *Can we please go over it again? This word "illusion"… we use it to call reality that was thought up by our brain in a certain way. Am I right?*

— This is what I call esoteric brain freeze. Pint came, and he says, "Everything you happen to be in is an illusion." Remove Pint and whatever he says, and everything will return to what it was before and become real again. Right? When Pint asks, "Why are you suffering from an illusory problem?" you don't tell him to go to hell only because you respect him. But nevertheless, if we were to remove Pint, everything would go back to normal, back to real.

— *We want to run away.*

— Yes, you find it unpleasant. Why does he call my life with all its worries, values, stresses, and anxieties illusory? Is he spitting on my life? Take a look inside and you will see these words there. You don't say it straight up, because you came, and you have paid for the seminar, but that's what you experience.

— *Why would we find it upsetting? Hmmm, illusion … Okay.*

119

— I judge based on the facts that I see. You stopped hearing what I say, and you immediately started to ask questions: "Why would we find it upsetting … Okay." Why aren't you listening?

— *I was listening.*

— You were listening, but do you hear what I say? That's the question. We can listen just because we have ears. But what enters these ears? What passes through them? And what remains in them? This is a big question. The fact that a human being has eyes does not necessarily mean that he sees. And the fact that he has ears does not necessarily mean that he hears.

— *We came to a stop when you asked us to name our key illusions.*

— *Yes, because it is impossible to call what is most important for me illusions.*

— You have believed in them your entire life.

— *The first thing I thought about was, "Health". Nothing can be done if you are not healthy. How can I call that an illusion?*

— Exactly. Nothing can be done unless you are healthy. You can't even listen to Pint if you are not healthy. You will not even get to Pint if you are not healthy. I have been trying and trying to get to him have a consultation with him, but I can't. That's what is real now! Take a look. These illusions are basic dualities.

— *First of all, the most painful illusions are those you believe in strongly. For example, "I will find a man and …I will have feelings … I will stop this fight between a man and a woman." And suddenly, I see that this fight will end.*

— *Another illusion is money. "I will be happy when I have enough money." That's what we believe.*

# To experience and to de-identify with the illusion of death

— You are attracted to this man because you don't have a man. You are preoccupied with money because you don't have enough money. You are preoccupied with health because you got sick. You are afraid of death because it is waiting for you.

Pint came here straight from a funeral. He just cremated his daughter. Is this another illusion?

— *I don't understand how one can see death as an illusion. How can one not become completely immersed in it?*

— He has cremated a daughter who was twenty-three years old.

— *How did she die?*

— How did she die? Who are you asking? Ask Pint how he went through this illusion. Look, Pint must go through every illusion that exists here, and he goes through them. The strongest illusion here is the illusion of death.

— *How can one go through this and see it as an illusion?*

— Where can you see illusions as illusions? When I, as a personage, think of my daughter … When I recall how we used to walk together … What she wanted … What do I immerse into? I immerse into tremendous grief. But when I enter another world and communicate with her Soul, I have a totally different perception. She died here having certain expectations. She died when she was just starting to live her own life. But when I move There and talk to her There, her Soul says, "I need to get out of here because I have to come back fast. This is the assignment of my Soul. I have finished my assignment in this body, and I have to enter another incarnation." In that case, this is not a hopeless suffering but a full understanding of what happens to the Soul and why it leaves the body. Look, death is the greatest illusion.

— *One has to have a clear understanding that nothing belongs to him.*

— Yes. I have played the role of a father here, while she played a role of a daughter. This was a show.

— *So, the greatest illusion here is life itself.*

— I am showing you, based on my own example, what it means to see an illusion as an illusion. I am showing you the role I am in. I am a father. Here is my daughter, and she is dying. She is not an old woman. She is my daughter, and children are expected to bury their parents here, not vice versa. But by understanding the meaning of this playground and understanding who we are and why we are here, I see it differently. This does not mean I don't experience this and I don't grieve for her. This is a paradox. I have spent three days in a state of total awareness, and I saw these transformations. In a state of identification, I have experienced grief. In a state of de-identification, I have experienced happiness. I went back and forth many times, observing the grandest illusion of this world—the illusion of death.

**There is a big difference between knowing that there is no death and experiencing it. I had to experience these states. This was a test for me. You have this knowledge, but will you be able to experience it this way, or will you experience it differently? This is the question.** My entire life was connected to death: to the death of people dying around me and to the death of betrayal. This is the illusion I must thoroughly investigate here—the death of the three closest human beings to me: my father, my mother, and my grandmother. That was horrible. But at the time, I did not understand what I understand now. This was horror, and this horror got fixed in me. Now, I was given a test: you know this, but how will *you* live through this?

Israel's seminar happened to be a preparation for this. This is very interesting. According to Mayan calendar, Israel's seminar took place during the time of the House of death. So, Israel's seminar was a preparation. I went through this Golgotha while we were there. I went to the bazaar and the church next to it where Jesus screamed at the merchants and turned over their tables. Both places are still active. They converted this place into something mundane and material. There is nothing else there. I was going through this loud bazaar, and at the same time I was going through something else. I was going through love and the total absence of love at the same time—just a bazaar. I saw what a Jew is. This was very important for me because I have been through many Jewish incarnations. So, what is a Jew? I saw that a Jew is love. But at the same time, the scariest thing for a Jew is to be loved. This is what he rejects the most. He does not want to feel who he really is. He does not want to feel that he is love.

— *Is he afraid of love?*

— Yes. Israel is a small model of Earth, where there is a constant war between Jews and Arabs. It is endless. No one understands it. This is a model of this playground in a very small territory. And as I was walking through this bazaar, I was thinking, "The House of Death is ending." And on the last day of the House of Death, my daughter died. This was a preparation. This was my preparation to experience death as illusion. This is very hard. I keep telling you, "In order for Pint to receive what he receives, he needs to experience everything this playground has to offer." He must walk through everything Earth offers. And afterwards, he receives the vision he discusses with you.

— *So, your life does not get easier.*

— **Life does not get easier. That's for sure.** When I look at my life, I can say only one thing: "I experience a certain relief when

I finish a task. I am able to relax for a short period of time, and then another assignment comes." I am not looking for some ephemeral happiness here. I know I am here to pass my lessons. And I know that these lessons are going to get harder and harder. This is my Way, and this is the way it is. I have never hidden it from anyone.

So, do you have enough courage to walk this way? Moreover, to have courage is not enough here. You need to have tools, and you must start seeing. You must walk into these illusions equipped with the ability to see illusions as illusions. You are entering a labyrinth. Will you be able to get out of it? You don't know. But you enter it. That's the way I enter these illusions.

Now look at your life and you will see which illusions in which you happen to be. What are the major labyrinths you are moving through now? These labyrinths will hold you until you see them as labyrinths, until you see the schematic plans of these labyrinths. Only then will you be able to exit. If you continue to run around these labyrinths scared, you will become more entangled. We just discussed the illusion of "Love" with Zoey. A labyrinth called "Love". How can you get out of it? You can only get out of it when you fully understand how it's made.

# We must understand the role of every actor of the show

— *There were a couple of personages in this labyrinth. I played one of them. Do I need to understand the thoughts, feelings, experiences, and motives of every player in order to get out of this labyrinth?*

— Yes. You need to understand the whole show. You need to understand the **script** of the entire show. It is not enough to know the role you played. You need to know and understand the role of every player of the show, and the meaning and structure of this entire script. Because, in reality, *you* are this show. It appears to you that you are just a role in this show, while actually, it appears to you that this is not a show. But this is a show where you play only one physical role, yet at the same time this show with every actor is you. But you cannot play all these roles while in this physical body and in this physical world. You can only understand this labyrinth, this game, by understanding every player and the mechanism based on which they pronounce their lines and complete their actions. They all support each other in this one unified action.

— *Will it help me to feel another participant of the show if I were to recall a situation when I was playing his or her role?*

— Of course. That's exactly how our following reincarnations occur. In one show you play a Jew, and in another you play a Nazi. But, in reality, you are both of them. This is your show. So, can you step away from the stage and look at the entire show? Can you see what happens to both actors and why it is happening?

— *Does it manifest itself in this incarnation too? Both the Nazi and the Jew?*

— These games are performed in different costumes and in different contexts, but the mechanisms are identical.

— *One has to catch the essence of the game, right?*

— Correct. Take a slave and a slave driver. Take a Nazi and a Jew in a concentration camp. These are two different backgrounds and totally different wardrobes, but the mechanism is the same.

— *Can I please get back to my show? I really want to sort it out. There are three actors. One of them is my husband. And at a certain point, he finds out that he is being betrayed by his wife. He feels betrayed. He feels jealousy, and he wants to avenge himself.*

— Great. But does he see how he betrays *her*? This is very important. You are looking at this show from one side. Do you see how this husband of yours betrays his wife, when you talk about a husband who is being betrayed? If you look at this show from one side, you will see that. And this vision will neutralize them in you. This is the key moment you must understand in order to de-identify with a given role.

— *Is his betrayal of her based on a different parameter? So, the personage feels himself cheated in one way, but he himself cheats based on a different parameter.*

— Exactly. It appears to the mind that he is being cheated on. She is physically with another man. But let's take a look at how *he* betrays her.

— *He does not give her feelings. He talks about feelings, but he does not give her any.*

— Exactly. He talks about love, but he does not give her love. He just keeps her on a leash. Instead of love, he gives her money. Isn't this cheating? But can he claim to be wronged if he behaves the same way toward her? Does he understand that?

— *He does not understand it as a personage. He cannot even connect these two things.*

— Exactly. The personage who plays the role of your husband does not know that, but you know that now. Both of these roles are yours. When you start to see more than the personage who plays in your show …

## Experiencing the situations and being tested on all three centers

— *This is a question I wanted to ask for a long time. Even when I am able to de-identify from a role and to see what's really happening, my personage still*

126

*gets "dragged into" the scene. When I look at it from above, my personage does not believe me.*

— That means that the lesson has not been mastered yet. What you call understanding is not a true understanding. You are just approaching this understanding. As you continue to work with it, you will experience a strong resistance. This resistance is necessary for you to understand your lesson.

— *I have heard that we are being tested three times, and then we are given a human being to whom we have to transmit this knowledge.*

— This is true.

— *Are we being tested on three centers?*

— *No. You will be given three situations, and you will experience each situation differently every time. When the same situation recurs, you will see it, and you will not be pulled into it again.*

— Three tests. Three tests of each center. Let's take a look at this. If we review this based on the death of my daughter, this was a test of my physical center. First, there was a preparation of the mental center. It was followed by a heavy emotional center experience in Israel, and only then the physical experience was offered.

— *So, your mental center was first to experience it?*

— **Yes, you will not be able to understand anything without the mental center. I am discussing it mentally with you now. We must sort out the intricate details of this mechanism. You are listening to me, and you are hearing me mentally. Later, once you come to understand it mentally, you will have to experience it emotionally. Only then will the third step come: this will have to be realized physically. When you experience this situation physically in a new way, you will understand it. That's when de-identification will occur. De-identification always occurs on three centers: mental, emotional, and physical. This is total de-identification. Otherwise, your de-**

127

identification is partial. You can mentally understand what I say, but at the same time you feel and do something entirely different. The inertia of these centers is enormous.

— *Hmmm, what does the absence of understanding lead to? It leads to anxiety, depression, and diseases of the physical body.*

— That's exactly what I tell you all the time. Both emotional and physical pain are the result of not understanding. A disease should be treated by understanding, not by medications. But there is almost no understanding here. You are meeting situations that you cannot understand. I am offering you a point of view, a vision, which will allow you to understand what's going on here.

— *This is very difficult to sort out!*

— What did you expect? We are talking about millions of past lives. Do you want us to sort it all out in five minutes? **We are not talking about how you are going to experience it in a state of "sleep", but how you are going to experience it coming out of sleep. The only way you can exit this sleep is by getting this knowledge. During the next step, this knowledge will have to be tested emotionally, and then physically. When all three components have been tested, the dream turns into illusion. Only then will you start seeing illusion as illusion.**

— *I have mentaly sorted out a certain situation. Now I have entered and experienced emotional pain. So, the next step will be physical, and then de-identification. Am I correct?*

— Yes. I tell you, "This is an illusion." You sort of agree with me mentally. Now I say, "Take Pint away." So? What happens? It's gone. You are back to normal. You are back to sleep. But when the level of your knowledge increases, you will start to see the discrepancy between this knowledge, your emotional states, and your physical actions. Do you understand? Everything here goes through dualities and conflict. Nothing will happen without you accumulating a certain amount of this knowledge, but this knowledge should transfer into a corresponding experience.

I again will bring up the experience of my daughter dying. My first reaction was the reaction of a "sleeping" man. After a certain period of time, it started to change; I started to experience change in the emotional center. It took me three days to balance all three centers, and this process still goes on. Once all three centers correspond with each other, this situation will finally transform into illusion.

— *Every one of us has experienced the opening of the emotional center, but ... what happens here? A certain knowledge accumulates. We come to the point when we need to experience it, but there are no feelings ... I don't get it?!*

— **This is a very difficult moment. This knowledge can convert into awareness. When this happens, you start to "hammer" others with it. You don't want to move to the emotional center. In some of you, it is totally closed, as we can see. In order for this knowledge to get down to the emotional center, the emotional center should be opened. It can only open through a heavy pain. You will meet with these kinds of situations when you have closed it. You have closed it when pain was intolerable. You need to open it.**

— *How can I get there? There are so many doors there.*

## Acquiring the tools of the self-investigator

— *Can I say something? I clearly saw this in Israel. I submerged into a state of "needed—not needed" when I was there. This state is connected to my mother. Does she need me or not? I have always felt mentally and emotionally that my dad needed me, and my mom did not. And when I thought about my mom, I always felt numb. I have never experienced any feelings toward her. None. I only*

129

*felt that I owe her something. I only felt indebted to her. And when I submerged into this state, I was shocked by the experience of "not being needed". I recalled a scene when my mother was in bed, dying. She was saying goodbye to me, telling me I was responsible for everything now. I was crying. I did not see anything that happened afterwards. But when I re-experienced this scene in Israel, the seminar's energy helped me to see what happened next. I was shaking. This "needed—not needed" duality was harshly intensified, but I did not move away from this pain. I allowed it to go all the way up. I have always thought she did not need me. But when I was sorting this out with Yolita, we concluded that when a human being dies, he always calls for the closest human being.*

*And I saw that Mom loved me dearly. I saw that she needed me. As a result, I was flipped into this "needed" part, and that allowed me to see the end of that scene. I saw Dad walking in. He approached the bedside table which held Mom's small medicine bottles, and he kicked it with his foot saying, "It's enough already. Stop bullying the kid. Take a look at the state you brought the child into." It was at that time that I said to myself, "I will not feel anymore. If I continue to feel this, Mom will die." And I stopped feeling. This was my key moment, "I will not feel. Otherwise, those who I am responsible for will die." This is what I recalled... I allowed myself to experience this state. It was painful, but I did it.*

*— And when you were in this state, you experienced love toward your mom and hatred toward your dad, which you did not know before.*

*— I am just starting to feel ... This is an early stage. I understand there is much more to come.*

— This is how it happens. You are trying to sort it out mentally: "What's going on? What can I do?" And suddenly, you are speeding down a very steep mountain. You are moving very fast. These are two totally different states: you standing on top of a mountain, and you speeding down this mountain. You cannot understand anything until you start to roll down this mountain. You can only have some philosophical discussions. That's why I say that until you start to roll down … Zoey and Dina … whether they decided to give the permission or not … That's it! They are rolling down!

— *I want to elaborate on how this permission gets born. I think every one of us has experienced a situation he constantly returns to in his thoughts. Every time you return there, you understand that something very important is buried there. Finally, you give yourself permission to enter this zone.*

— Exactly. Every time I go to the dentist, I am in excruciating pain. I will not go otherwise. I must be in excruciating pain … We are dealing with a similar thing here. When your tooth is not hurting, you can contemplate, "Should I go or not?"

— *So, should we wait for the pain to become unbearable?*

— No. You should not wait. You are getting tools here. You will either go down this mountain, hitting every tree on your way, or you will learn to use the tools I am offering you. Why do I keep telling you, "Webinars, seminars, and daily School work are necessary"? Because when the time will come for you to go down this mountain, you will be able to navigate your way down. You will either roll down this mountain, hitting everything on your way, or you will ski down it in a professional skier-suit equipped with the best skis and ski poles money can buy, knowing how to use this equipment. Do you understand the difference?

That's what we do here. We acquire these tools. Eventually, this painful situation will recur, and you will either close down again, or you will start to ski down the slope knowing what you are doing. I know that. I have been through everything you are going through. You have already started to understand that our Process is not something uncontrollable, while a man who is not equipped with this knowledge wants only one thing—to get away from this pain, not to look in its direction.

— *My intellectual center knows that I feel happiness while I have to feel sorrow. I have started to see both states in me. Initially, I felt that I have these*

131

*states. I am just not aware of them. I always observe my thoughts. I allow myself to observe the most horrible thoughts from the matrix point of view. But I do not allow myself to experience difficult emotional states. I am not aware of my emotional data base at all.*

— Sooner or later, everyone in the Process will experience the need to move to the emotional center. When this happens, you will have to get in touch with something similar to what Zoey is touching now. But she acquired the tools, and she can now enter it. Yes, it is painful. Yes, it is hard. But this is the way our Process is going.

— *I have this feeling now. I understand that I am in the beginning or in the middle of this situation, but I feel sure I will be able to get out of it.*

— You will be able to get out of everything you encounter. Everyone who enters this Process will get everything he needs. Every time you attend a webinar or a seminar, you receive what you need.

— *I want to ask for your help. Can you please kick me? I cannot climb this mountain on my own. I turn away from it.*

— What kind of a kick do you want from me? **You need to work and acquire the tools I urge you to acquire. Otherwise, you will roll down this mountain just as I explained it to you. We are entering hard times. Very strong currents of energy have started to move.**

Take a look around you. Look at Japan. Look at the Middle East. We are entering the testing grounds called "Quantum Leap 2012". It has started already. These energies get stronger and stronger, and they exacerbate everything. Many people will leave based on the choice their Soul will make. Some will participate in the Process and move on, others will stay here. We have entered the Process that most people don't know about and don't even want to know about. But whether they know about it or not, they participate in it. You can see it by watching the news, even though no one explains it this way.

The Japanese have completely suppressed their feelings, and the country is being shaken. The explosion at the nuclear power plant was not a coincidence. These things happen in certain places and in certain nations. It has to do with the National ego structure. But similar explosions occur in every ego-personality. Are you going to wait for your power plant to explode, or will you start to work on yourself?

What we are dealing here is similar to the Russian revolution. Do you understand? There are Reds and there are Whites. And some people want to sit in the kitchen and stay out of it. What happens? Red comes, and they shoot those who want to stay out. Then Whites come, and they shoot them too. You have to decide who to go with. But what does personality want? It wants to stay in a warm place. But try to understand. We are entering the irreversible process. Things will never be the same. The times we are in offer enormous opportunities for all of us, and first of all, for the Souls that are present here. That's what my daughter said to Yolita: "I am leaving so I can return and meet the knowledge Dad carries." She could not do it in the body she was in. That's how the Soul carries out its plan sometimes. This body and this incarnation represent a certain stage for a Soul. When this stage is over, another starts.

## Solving the equation inside yourself

*— I have a question. My emotional center started to open up after the April seminar. I have met a man. I have experienced very strong feelings toward him. I was barely able to sustain them. My husband found out about him three months ago. I've been crying non-stop ever since. There was this sense of duty on one side and very strong feelings on the other side. I have been suffering emotionally and physically all this time. Both of them have suffered too. One started to drink. The other was admitted to the hospital with a heart condition. I decided to leave my*

*family, and I am leaving with my new boyfriend now. This happened in December. But I continue to experience this feeling of guilt for leaving my husband and kids. I am trying to sit on two chairs now. I keep running between the two of them. I feel crucified. I have started to see certain things while I have been experiencing this emotional and physical stress. I want to find out whether this was my own request.*

*I am very close to my father emotionally. My mom is an intellectual. I intended to get to know and to understand my dad and to see all of this through somehow. I started to understand that all these crazy feelings, two men, jealousy ... all of this belongs to my dad's side ... it was hidden from me. I also saw this crazy-aggressor-oppressor part of me. It can kill. When I saw this, I experienced gratitude for seeing myself. The question I have is, "Does me seeing this really reduce these emotions?" I can see now that I am going to go for a second round of this. And I see that I have created all of this. But these emotions do not disappear. I don't know whether I can handle them.*

— First of all, you have to understand that these two men represent two opposite parts of you. Can you describe them using words? One side is your husband. Let's call this side, "duty and family". What word can we use to name the other part?

— *Feelings?*

— Correct. A very strong fight occurs between duty-family part of you and your emotional-physical part. This show, which is quite dramatic by the way, was created in order for you to be able to harmonize these two parts. You cannot reject one side. If you do that, the situation will continue. You need to get these two parts in contact inside of you. What does one part know about the other part? They need to get to know each other, and you need to find balance.

— *So, this is the way for them to get in touch with each other. And the only way they can do it is through conflict. That is the only way they know.*

— Actually, if we look at it from the survival standpoint, they want to destroy each other. If we look at it from the point of view of

134

the Process in which you participate, it is truce and partnership. Can you bring these two parts to partnership? If you were to reject mother-kids part and move to the sex-feelings part, you would experience a colossal feeling of guilt. If you were to reject sex and feelings and move to the mother part, you would experience strong condemnation. Can you combine these two parts and see both of them inside you? Can you equalize and bring these two parts to partnership inside yourself?

The role of mother-duty does not presuppose sexual and emotional manifestations. A mother's role is to take care of her children. Can you combine this role with wild sexuality? You must have an actor who will manifest it. But in this case, you don't need the mother part. In this case, kids are just an obstruction. You don't need this mother-duty part.

Take a good look at this. This is a very strong stretch of a duality. These roles cannot be combined in the usual sense. You can only bring them together through inner work. This is not easy. As you can see, the first act of this show is quite dramatic. The second act repeats the first act, but it is less dramatic. But the level of drama and what you are going to come to as a result of this show depends on the work you are going to do. I am showing you what's going on. Can these two parts coexist? Can you not condemn yourself when you are in these two parts?

— *I was thinking about it … All these states …I can say now that I accept the mother-duty part in me. I also accept sensuality. I can really say that I accept myself in all these manifestations. But in order to do that, I had to enter each of these parts separately and to see their necessity and kaif.*

— Yes. They are equally necessary, equally important, and equally respected.

— *It seems to me there is no contradiction in being in both of them simultaneously.*

*— I had an illusion that I accept all of this, but external mirrors reflect what happens inside us. At one point, my husband agreed with me about going to another man, and I had an illusion that the situation calmed down. I thought everything was going to be okay … I thought I accepted it inside … and all of this is going to be okay and quiet … and suddenly, there was a huge explosion! It turned out that nothing was accepted, and nothing was brought to partnership.*

— Yes. We have to consider the specifics of these scenarios. Take Romeo and Juliet. Would they experience this crazy love if their clans were not feuding with each other? These strong feelings and emotions appear only in lieu of very strong prohibitions. Would they be so strong if we were to take the prohibitions away? No. That's why this type of "love," the "love" our classics love to write about, is always dramatic and almost always ends in death.

*— I start to attract lovers into my life when my relationship with my husband starts to cool off.*

— And then your whole understanding of "love" changes. You suddenly start to strive for some kind of passion. A woman irons and cooks for her family with her eye on the TV, where passions are being played out.

*— Yes, I dream about being that woman on the screen …*

— This idea is very stable. I cannot realize it here, in this reality, but I will watch a show tonight, and I will have a dream about being Angelica, Marquise of the Angels. You can laugh, but this is the way it is. That's why I keep telling you that the equalization of these things will bring you to experience a serious drop in those states. You will not be able to get so "excited". You will get to the calm, neutral zone.

*— My grandmother used to say, "The biggest foolishness lovers can do is to get married."*

— Lovers should meet at night. They should write letters and sprinkle perfume on them.

*— Does your husband play the role of a lover now?*

— Yes, never forget about the opposite part. It must always be present. There was this handsome man. She ran to him, and they jumped into bed. And they sweated in each other arms having wild, passionate sex. And they sweated the next day, but they sweated a little bit less. And a week later they stopped sweating, and they started to think, "What is he doing here? What am I doing here? I have so many things to take care of at home." But for all of this to be hot, you have to have a situation. Someone has to be close to a heart attack. Someone has to collapse, screaming, "I am going to hang myself!" Someone has to have sex while feeling dirty and disgusting, and getting increasingly excited because of it. What will happen if you were to take this away? You would come home, and he would be sitting there drinking his tea and asking, "Where have you been? Oh, you saw your lover. How is he doing?"

— *Yes. They come from work, have their dinner, and go to bed. All quiet. But let them have a fight, and it is followed by wild sex.*

— Take a look at how much you need this crazy sex! But in order to have it, you need to have a background and a context. So, what do you need? Do you need harmonization or wild sex? Do you need to realize your notion about a woman's happiness? Do you need to realize your notion about the wild happiness of a woman and the wild unhappiness of the same woman?

— *Sprinkled with wild sex.*

— So, take a look and see that these ideas exist, and they are quite strong in you: "I want some wild sex with a muscular black guy on a roof of a skyscraper in Miami." We are being fed these pictures all the time. Take a look around you: TV, billboards, etc. You don't even discern them! The happiness of the other family side is the happiness of a wallet. The wildest family happiness is a supermarket sale. It's the pinnacle of the unification of family members.

137

You are laughing, but this is all around you: on every wall, on every TV channel. And it gets fixated in you. You cannot resist it. You realize this without any awareness of where this is coming from. I am going to sprinkle this perfume on my neck, and thousands of men will love me to death. You are laughing, but this is in your heads because this is everywhere! And it requires realization! Then you ask, "What's happening to me?"

*— I saw something interesting recently. I saw that in the same situation, let's say at work, I can perceive people as my oppressors, and at the same time I can see myself as their oppressors. Everything depends on my point of view. I don't understand who sees that. Personality should not be able to see that. So, who chooses this point of view?*

## Your experience and understanding of the situations accelerates when you are in the Process

— Personality cannot see it. It is fixed in one side. Even what we call changes here are fixed. You were a communist and you fought priests before. You suddenly flipped, converted, and became a priest. You will fight communists now. By changing your side, you still keep condemnation and guilt. Only the Supreme Aspect can see that. When you start seeing things out of the Supreme Aspect, when you experience very fast changes in that point of view, personality starts to go crazy, because it starts to lose itself. Personality only exists when it is in one side and condemns the other.

*— I think my Observer sees mentally. It follows that in order to enter and experience this oppressor, I need to get into the game and enter a state. Am I right?*

138

— We experience everything partially here. Can you see that you oppress in the same way you are being oppressed? You don't. You don't experience the state of the oppressor. We are returning to the topic of three centers again. As you can see, this is not an easy subject. We finish up with the illusion when we see two opposite parts in all three centers.

This is the formula I repeat: "Three times two. Three centers in duality." Until you work the illusion through this formula, it will remain an illusion, even though you will have the illusion that you become aware of it. **This is awarishness, not awareness.** It prevents you from going further through the centers.

First, you need to sort out this illusion mentally. Then you need to experience it emotionally. And lastly, you need to experience it physically. Only then will you get out of it and it will stop bothering you. You will not think about it at all.

What does it mean, "Problem disappeared"? It means it doesn't exist. How does a problem appear? It's a thought. What regulates the appearance of thoughts in your head? Have you observed why these thoughts appear? Where do they come from?

— *It follows that I am in my intellectual center now. When I start to see my states and to experience them, I will be able to de-identify with them.*

— Exactly. These feelings and thoughts appear on your screen. As bubbles, they ascend from the states you have experienced and suppressed during your life. These states are preserved in sub-consciousness, but they produce bubbles. Suddenly, one of these bubbles pops to consciousness. This bubble comes from a situation that occurred twenty years ago. You think you have changed. You think you are different now. No. You continue to carry the baggage that are preserved there, and they continue to produce bubbles. These bubbles get registered on the conscious level as thoughts or states. You are sitting next to a person you love, and suddenly you

139

find yourself overwhelmed by a state of guilt or some unexplainable fear. You don't understand where these feelings and thoughts are coming from. The external environment does not show it. It's inside.

These bombs will continue to explode for no apparent reason until you demine this mine field. You don't know where these mines are buried. You need to find them and to demine them. You have buried these mines yourself, but you don't know where they are. You are walking a mine field, and you have no idea when and where the next mine is going to blow up. My work is akin to the work of a military de-miner. The mines are set at the different levels of your age. Most of them were set up in childhood.

— *This is very interesting. I dig into the story of my childhood mentally every day. When I come to see a certain situation, it repeats itself a couple of times. It sometimes realizes itself physically. I can walk through it and experience it emotionally. I get submerged into these states.*

— *That's what it is. Then you come to the surface and become aware of it.*

— Our Process provides a very strong acceleration. It offers you tools and allows you to see this. You can understand the situations you encounter. The time span you need to do this de-mining is not so long. People who are "asleep" spend years doing it. Years! And they don't understand anything. They don't see the connection between one side and the other. They are "asleep". The curve of their life is flat. The Process offers very strong fluctuations and big amplitude. It accelerates everything tremendously, which allows you to see things clearly. Having the knowledge and equipment of the de-minor, you start to do that. The "sleeping" man does not understand that he is dealing with mines. He does not understand that one of his own mines just detonated. And he cannot understand that because his consciousness works at a very slow speed, which does not allow him to see the interconnectedness of the opposites.

— *All of his energy is spent finding someone he can blame for what is happening to him.*

— Yes. This is the traditional gentleman's set.

— *A thought popped into my head yesterday, and I still cannot process it. My father, my son, and my neighbor … are they one?*

— Yes. This is your Soul. Most often this is the case. Your relatives represent one Soul, which agrees to come and meet in different incarnations to play out a certain show. We are playing different roles in different shows with these people. Today she is your daughter. In the last incarnation she could have played your wife or your mother.

— *I told you about the incarnation in which I killed a child. I recalled sticking a knitting needle into a child's heart and experiencing perverted pleasure out of it. And then it started, "Why don't I feel guilty? Why don't I condemn myself?" I felt good killing this child. He was sick, and I had the idea that sick people should be killed. I manifested aggression all day yesterday. I completely submerged into this killer yesterday! I did not care whether you understand me or not! I had to kill this not understanding in you!*

— The idea of racial cleansing was quite widespread amongst Germans during the mid-twentieth century. They developed a big theory around it. They had a big team of scientists working to determine who belongs to the Aryan race and who belongs to the lowest races. People who belonged to the lowest races were to be exterminated. This was the main idea of Hitler's Germany.

— *I don't remember the room. I don't remember anything. I only remember this pleasurable state I was in. It was similar to sexual pleasure.*

*Yesterday, when I started to manifest this aggression, I recalled something else. We had a sick child in our family. On a conscious level, I manifested two states: killing to cleanse, and a desire to help the sick member of my family. He was disabled, and I could not help him. And now, in this incarnation, I*

141

*simultaneously experience the desire to save my child and to kill him. This is condensed in time, and this is in me!*

*I did not know what to do this morning. I thought to myself, "Don't I have any desire to help?" I am living with this state of guilt for not being able to help my child for the past five years. All of this is in me: the desire to kill and the desire to save her.*

— We have another question: to help someone to live here or to help them die? Does a sick man have a right to die when he chooses to die, or should he die when a doctor says he can die? And what does a doctor do here? A doctor tries to resurrect him all the time. We have hospitals now where sick people have a right to die when they want to die, but it is the duty of a doctor to save them. Whether the doctor wants to or not, he will prolong a patient's life, even when the patient is suffering. These are the dilemmas that appear here during unilateral movement. We need to save him, so he can stay here. We should not save him. He should not be here. Two extremely opposite points of view. And then you have your doctor-killer.

— *So, one should not interfere.*

— Yes, but when a patient dies, the doctor may be held responsible. And it is taken for granted here that the doctor should save his patient and prolong his life. It's his duty to keep him here. His duty is not to send him There.

— *One of my sons was very emotional. If someone was to take a toy away from him, he would throw tremendous tantrums. If I was not fast enough, he would collapse, breathless. Then he would take a deep breath and wake up as if nothing has even happened, totally calm. There was some kind of shift from one reality to another.*

— This is fear, mindless fear of losing something. This game we play here is about survival, and this part is very strong in him: "I have to grab something, otherwise I will die."

142

*— When I left, he lost his mom. I tried to tear him away from me, so he would become independent.*

— You were something he was holding on to very strongly. He should have experienced it in this incarnation. As you can see, we are dealing with different Souls and different experiences here. His assignment, as we can see now, was, "Mine! Only mine! If you don't give it to me, I will die!" That's the way a Soul gets to know the other side of the experience. When a Soul comes here with such extremely manifested opposite qualities, it experiences tremendous difficulties. Look at these rich businessmen who commit suicide when they lose their money. This is their equivalent of the toy. I will kill myself if I lose my money. Or, I will kill myself if he leaves me. What will I live for if this is not mine?

But what is this "mine"? This is another question. Two women grab for a man, and this question becomes a life and death question for them: "This is mine—you can die, or this is yours—I will die." That's what we observe here quite often.

*— I can see now that I either save people or kill them. I have not experienced anything else.*

— You can't really kill anyone. You are either in this world or you There. You are a door man: stay here or go there.

*— After experiencing this aggression yesterday, I am experiencing guilt now. I feel guilty now for this murder. I might get dragged into that direction now.*

— Yes, you might. You need to get out of this illusion. You are dealing with a very strong stretch here. You are dealing with two opposite sides. It appears now that they are incompatible, but you need to combine them. You need to see white in black and black in white, and then you need to neutralize them.

When you get to the "zero" point of this duality, you will become neutral. This is where the exit out of the illusion of this duality lies. When you understand the "plus" of the negative, of what you have

143

considered to be negative, and the "minus" of the positive, you will equalize them. This is very difficult. You must experience it and combine it inside of you. It must happen on every level: intellectual notions, emotional states, and physical manifestations. The Process starts with the intellectual center, and then you experience this emotionally, and only then comes the physical realization. You get to "zero" when you complete the whole three-step process.

# CHAPTER 4
# RECREATION OF PERSONAL SCREENPLAYS

•◆•◆•◆•◆•◆•◆•◆•◆•◆•◆•◆•◆•◆•◆•◆•◆•◆•

## The endless run from happiness to unhappiness and back

*— Can I start? I tried to sort my situation out yesterday. I tried to see it using the analogy of two tennis rackets and a tennis ball you offered to Zoey. Her husband could not give her what she wanted, and she left him. For this, she experienced a feeling of guilt. But, on the other hand, no one is guilty here, because her husband has a different program—he could not give her what she needed.*

— Moreover, he was not supposed to give it to her. Please, try to understand that all these movements and betrayals are just the role-playing of this scenario, where everyone performs his role. He played the role: husband-kids-duty. And there was the opposite role there: sex-passion. These two roles cannot be combined. When a human being plays this role, he or she only plays this role. You cannot find everything in one store. If you need to buy bread, you go to a supermarket. If you want to buy furniture, you go to the store that sells furniture.

*— In that case, there is no guilt.*

— There is no guilt if you feel it that way. But the fact of the matter is that everyone who is involved in this game feels it. It appears that they betray, moving from one side to another. Look. You are eating soup, and then you stop. You put your spoon down, pick up a fork and knife and start eating a steak. Can we say that you betrayed soup for a steak? You are laughing, but we are dealing with the same thing here. However, people experience a very real feeling of guilt for betrayal.

— *Yes, that's the thought that popped into my head yesterday: "I did not betray him." He just could not give me what I needed. He was playing this role, and he continues to play it quite naturally. There is nothing to blame him for, and there is nothing to blame me for.*

— There is nothing to blame him for, and there is nothing to blame you for. But do you see it this way when being totally "asleep "you run toward one man or when you are being repelled from him? **This repulsion is stimulating you; it gives birth to condemnation, and condemnation gives birth to guilt.** Otherwise, this drama would mellow down. Everything that people do with horrible, contorted faces is being done calmly and quietly here. No one worries about anything here. Imagine a theater. People come to see a drama. They are supposed to cry and feel strong emotions, but everything is quiet. They quietly sat through the performance and they left quietly.

— *I have a question then. How can one see anything new if everything is nice and quiet? We have learned by now that something new can only be born through pain.*

— Yes, something new gets born through pain. But when it is born, the situation will be totally different. Are you ready for this birth? Are you ready to get off this drug dependency? Do you understand that this is the narcotic you use? You scream, "Guilt! Condemnation! I betrayed him! He betrayed me!" and your narcotic state escalates. What I discuss here is sobriety. There is none of it There. There is no passion and no sex There that would make you throw your husband and children away and to experience guilt and remorse afterwards. You run back feeling guilty, and you cry and cry and cry. Then you scream, "The hell with him," and you run back. Take a look at this. What do you need?

— *One side says, "I need this," but the other side says, "I don't".*

— Facts. Only facts will tell you whether you need it or not. If you calm down and sober up, the external manifestations will change. Moreover, your state will be totally different.

— *Will we not suppress and extinguish our emotions then?*

— If this is the way you see your emotions, considering that a human being should perish in the passion of sex, in the passion of duty, in the passion of responsibility — this is not the life for you. The life I discuss will offer emotions of different qualities. You will transfer to a totally different quality of perception.

Imagine you get a street dog. You pull him out of a vicious dog fight. He is covered in blood. You brought him home and cleaned him up. You fed him. He stayed with you for a week, and he recovered. What is he thinking? He is bored: "Where is the kaif? Where is the old smelly dumpster? Where is this bitch I should have..." Apply this to yourself, and you will see ...

— *I was experiencing a very unusual state before the New Year, a state of unusual calmness. My mind could not appraise it. I felt quiet and calm. And I felt nervous after a while. Suddenly, I felt I was lacking something!*

— What was considered to be the most horrible thing during the era of Socialism? It was indifference. If you watch the movies of that era, you will see people puffing up with pride and screaming about their truth. They had to fight for their truth! And what about a guy who does not participate in all of this? No one sees him. He is indifferent to what's going on. He can't even fall in love. He is very mellow. Some hero falls in love and breaks everything around him for love, but this guy ... what would people say about him? They would say, "He is indifferent. He does not have any emotions."

*— And we start to search for these emotions. They are so habitual for us. We can't find them here.*

*— Emotions don't disappear. You can experience happiness. But such states as guilt and pity disappear.*

**— You are trying to use a psychological classification now: emotions, feelings, etc. Let's not do that. Psychologists have been arguing trying to separate and define them for decades. Let's use one word to describe all of them: states.**

**Fear splits into condemnation, guilt, and pity. That's it. All other feelings derive from these three states. Everything else is just a derivative.** When you remove this root cause, all other feelings change. They totally transform. There is no point in talking about it, because any word I say will be used by you in accordance with the corresponding-to-it experience you have in your library. I, on the other hand, discuss the experience you do not yet possess. It is not in your library yet.

The entire experience that comes from fear and that later splits into condemnation, guilt, and pity has these shades. Take happiness for example. You are wearing a nice dress, and you look good today. A certain young man is paying you more attention than he pays to your girlfriend, and that makes you happy. Can we use this word "happiness" to describe this state? What's behind this happiness? And take "Happiness of returning home." The word we use is the same: "happiness". But how different are the states that stand behind this word! Words play the role of the pointers, and the direction they point us toward is frequently not very clear.

I say a word, and I mark my state with it. You hear this word, but it means something totally different to you. It is hard to find words to describe the feelings that I discuss when I discuss this state of a sober, vigilant, awake human being. There are no words for them in our "sleeping" vocabulary. We are entering unknown territory. I enter the unknown every day during a seminar. I don't know. Then, after I've lived through and experienced something, I can lean on it. But if I were to continue to prolongate what I know, I will not experience anything new.

The "sleeping man" wants to have the same thing over and over again. He has something on a shelf, and he wants to have more of it. He has a cup on his shelf with a tag: "Happiness". It contains five grams of something. He says, "I have to fill it up." He does not have enough. He wants to pour everything from the cup "sorrow" into the cup of "happiness". That's what he does. He thinks he can do it. This is what I call an illusion.

**Take a look at what you are striving for now. Let's call it "woman's happiness". What is it? You wake up in the morning, and you don't feel woman's happiness. After lunch you feel full, but you still don't feel woman's happiness. Dinner comes and still no woman's happiness. But everywhere around you—on the TV screen, in the magazines, on the advertisement billboards—you are being shown the examples of this so-called woman's happiness, and you run toward these examples. They are not you. They are being shown to you, but you cannot reach it. If you reach and experience it, it will disappear. You can only desire what you don't have. And the bigger your deficit of something, the stronger your desire for this something is going to be. This is not just a desire. This is a desire "to desire". The aim is not important. What's important is your state—the state that I call the "desire to desire". But when you finally reach what you desire, this state will disappear. In this way, without even understanding it, you maintain this state. When finally, you get to experience this desire of yours, you will be able to say, "This is it?! This is love?! Is this it?! Is this love?!"**

— *It flips into hate.*

— Exactly. But flipped into hate, you will strive back toward love again. This is a paradox. A Perpetua mobile. This will continue to happen until you experience it and understand what you were striving for. This process is accompanied by a state of depression and loss of meaning. You experience total emptiness.

When someone who has just graduated from a PhD program or medical school is asked what he feels, the usual reply is, "I don't feel anything. I feel empty." This is what he strived for. It seems to us he should feel happy. But he feels total emptiness. Then he needs to find something else. A human being constantly needs to desire something. Once he realizes something, he needs to start running toward something else. He cannot enjoy what he has.

— *This is a state of aspiration. One gets energy there. Without an aim, you don't have anything.*

— Exactly. So, the state of the "desire to desire" is an energy source, not the aim by itself.

— *Yes, because the mechanisms are different. Some don't reach their goals at all in order to maintain this state. Others have to set up a new aim as soon as they reached their goal. And they do that until they totally exhaust themselves. The essence is the same.*

— And someone dies when he achieves his aim. Take a look at Alexander the Great. He conquered the whole world and died. He could not conquer the moon.

So, this is how the machine of a "sleeping" man works, but he is not aware of it. So, can you receive pleasure from your desires?

— *One can receive pleasure from it, but then one will face the question, "What energy am I going to live on now?" In order to live, I need energy, and I produce this energy from the desire to get something or from the desire to escape something.*

150

# Personal program has many levels of complexity

— It appears to you that a human being produces this energy. In reality, a human being is just a product of this matrix, which is built this way. You are looking at the computer screen and playing a certain game. There are many personages in this game. You are looking at the personage that you chose for this game. He is running non-stop. He jumps up and down. Someone attacks him. Who is doing this? Is he doing this? You understand that this is a preprogrammed personage, which moves according to the screenplay created for this game. I had a very interesting experience yesterday. I suddenly saw all of this as a 3D animation. I was a personage in this animation.

But then we should ask ourselves a question: "Who controls this personage?" The personage thinks he is the one who does it.

— *This's not true! The program controls him!*

— That's right. And who controls the program? This is mind blowing. Everything is clear and well understood when we talk about an animation, but what if you yourself are one of the personages of this animation?

— *You are inside a program. This is it.*

— But why don't you want to search for the one who has created this program? Who controls this program? Who is leading you? What is the aim of this program? There are so many questions here.

Look at the enormous animation called "Earth" now. So many programs must be coordinated! Seven billion people organized into nations, states, organizations, etc. All of them interact somehow. Who navigates all of this? All of this has meaning and purpose. Don't you find it fascinating?

*— So, who controls all of this? I understand that this is a program. I, the personage with a name Svetlana, came here to carry out this program, and I stupidly perform what I am supposed to perform, experiencing guilt and condemnation. When I am awake enough to observe something, I observe. Initially, pride would not allow me to do that: "What do you mean? Am I some kind of an ant in a program that I cannot get out of?!" But it really holds you tight. It seems to you, you did something against the program, but pretty soon you realize you are just fooling yourself. I kept asking, "Why is this the way it is? Why? How?" Finally, I came to understand that there is some kind of a Supreme Consciousness, which sends its robots here to obtain certain results. We accumulate a certain experience here and then we return, loaded with it. That's what I understood, and I started to ask myself, "What is my Assignment?" Is it to experience "Loneliness"? It calmed me down, and I experienced it differently.*

— You are just sitting there looking at the women and wondering, "Why are they running around? Why are they so anxious? I feel good. I feel lonely!"

*— Yes. I understand that this is my program. What is there to be anxious about? You can't get out of it anyway.*

— My girlfriend will sleep with her husband for the rest of her life, but I am given to experience loneliness and a cat.

*— Is this not so?*

— That's what you are telling us.

*— Yes. It appears to me that I have done something new, but in reality, I do the same thing over and over again.*

— Okay. Let's take a look at Pint. He is also a program. But his program is a bit unusual. He can't live the way other people live. He understands that he is a program. Why doesn't he live like Svetlana? Why can't he just live quietly. No, he must gather people around him and start to wake them up. Why can't he live according to his program? Why does he try to figure out something? What is this self-investigation?

— *So what is Pint saying? Can one jump out of the program?*

— *I think he is saying that by seeing this program and by working through it, one can achieve some kind of freedom.*

— You just started to understand the predetermined nature of the program, and your legs got weak: "We can't jump out of it!" But Pint is talking about something else.

— *Did you say one can jump out of the program?*

— Finally, after ten years!

— *One can experience it differently. What do I observe now? I observe myself and my sister. Certain things happen to us at the same time. I understand that this is our program. But there is a slight difference here: I experience it differently. My perception is different.*

— *We are still going to be in it, right?*

— *In my case, this is what it is now.*

— *Can someone explain to me whether I can get out of this program or not? The way I understand it, once you see your program, you acquire the necessary experience you were supposed to acquire during your lifetime much faster, and then you go for a holiday.*

— *Okay, I am a program. I understand that. Does it mean I have to experience this script for the rest of my life? I don't get it.*

— Let's try to figure this out. This is very important.

— *Does this program consist of every situation and every duality that we are supposed to experience here?*

— *It is the experience you need to acquire, and not only during this lifetime, but in many lifetimes. I accrue a certain experience. It was very difficult for me to accept that I will not be able to jump out of this program. But first of all, when I came to know that, my perception changed; I can experience this mess differently now. Moreover, it turned out, there are many things I have not ever noticed before. We can see this as a change in the program, or as the acquisition of a new experience. That's what happened to me. My experience is changing.*

— Let's take a look at the Rubik's cube we are all familiar with. You mix everything up, and then you need to arrange it in a certain way. Every time you mix it up, you receive a new configuration. And you are dealing with a difficult puzzle every time, but the Rubik's cube is the same. Take a look at your program from this point of view.

*— There is another problem here. One gets stuck with a certain experience at a certain age, and one continues to accrue this experience until one becomes aware of it. One can only move forward when one's perception of this experience changes.*

— Let's go further. You have configured this Rubik's cube a certain way, and you get stuck; you cannot solve this puzzle for three weeks. Finally, you solve it. Then, you mix it all up again and you get to a new configuration. Until you sort many of these puzzles and understand what this cube is about, you will not be able to solve these puzzles fast. When you have gone through many different puzzles, you lose interest in the whole thing.

The personal program we are dealing with is similar to this Rubik's cube that is being transformed. The program has many levels. You can get stuck on one level and spend many lives solving one puzzle. Then, when you get to a new level, you encounter a more complicated assignment. As you can see, your program has many levels and many assignments. The program stays the same, but reviewing it on a different level offers you a new assignment.

## Past life recall. Why is it necessary?

*— I came home yesterday, and as I was putting my child to bed I experienced tremendous gratitude. I already know this state of total acceptance. I have experienced the state of gratitude toward everyone but you, Svetlana. It's interesting, because whenever I happen to be in personality, I feel great sympathy*

*toward you. I don't know what this is connected to. I've already experienced a similar situation in Israel.*

*Finally, I got into a certain state where I realized that we've met somewhere in our past lives, and we are somehow connected. As I worked on it, I realized that I feel very guilty around you. Previously, I experienced strong aggression toward you, to the point that I wanted to kill you. I experienced this same aggression yesterday. It is connected to the state of pregnancy and process of delivery somehow. I think I project something onto you, but I don't know exactly what. If you are ready to discuss it, I invite you to do it now. We have never looked at your request to get married and to have children from this angle.*

*I saw that I was a reason … there was a pregnant woman there, and she knew that when she would deliver her baby, the baby would be taken away, and she would be killed. Some kind of a scientific experiment was conducted there, and she was a part of it. I saw myself killing this woman.*

*When I started to experience gratitude and acceptance toward everyone, I realized that you were excluded. And then I saw a whole set of these pictures.*

— What do I have to do? Tell me.

— *Do you have this fear? Do you have this fear of giving birth? What is your perception of all of this? If you want me to, I can describe this picture in detail. But what if it's mine? What if I am projecting something onto you?*

— Don't worry about it. Keep talking.

— *This is not a coincidence. I must do this. I felt very guilty about it in that previous incarnation. But if I were to refuse, I would be killed. There were many pregnant women there. They were experimented upon.*

— What kind of time frame were you in? Was it Nazi's Germany?

— *It looks like it was. I see myself in a military outfit.*

— They did quite a few experiments on pregnant women. Are you a man there?

— *No, I am a woman.*

— Is it a concentration camp?

155

*— I am not sure. It's a big place. There are prisoners there. Some experiment is being conducted on them. Women are being raped. They get pregnant. And then these people in military outfits conduct experiments on these women and their babies. The subject of their interest is how mothers would experience their babies being killed. How would they survive that? And this woman knows what awaits her. She is afraid to deliver. She knows that this will be the starting point of her suffering.*

— Who are these women? Are they Jewish?

*— There are many women there. They are of different nationalities.*

— Who are those people conducting the experiments?

*— They are Nazis. They want to learn something about the mother-child relationship.*

— What do they need this information for?

*— They want to know how the defense system is going to operate: will she try to save herself or her child?*

— What do they need this information for?

*— I don't know that. I am just a small screw in this machine. I am just an average worker.*

— Are you a guard there?

*— I think I am. And I don't feel any kaif doing it. I am forced to do that. Otherwise, I will be shot. I do it out of fear. I am terribly scared. I know I will pay for it later.*

— Your recollection is not coincidental. Let's take a look at your current life. Your kids are constantly sick. You are experiencing something similar to what that woman experienced. You need this recollection in order to understand and to equalize the experience you currently have.

*— I wanted to discuss it today for two reasons. My program did not change, but I can see it from two different angles now. I allow myself to recall things now. I experience terrible fear when I talk to you. The way I see it now, this is my*

156

*rejection of the fear of craziness. It does not matter to me how you will perceive me. I feel what is important. This is my reality now.*

*— I can't recal anything.*

— This is irrelevant now. What's relevant now is that you talk, Dina. You must enter it and extract everything you can extract out of it. The door is open. You need to enter it.

*— I started to experience this aggression and the feeling of guilt. I started to experience these players from different sides.*

— What we discuss is connected to my Rudolf incarnation. He was a Nazi, too. He did not like what was going on, but he could not change anything. He used to go on very difficult assignments. Then he was thrown into a concentration camp. He could not understand anything. He used to see these people as enemies, and suddenly he turned into one of them. Can you imagine the state he was in? What was life worth at that time? And my daughter's death is connected to this, too. All of this is very important. I extracted everything I could out of it. I can feel Rudolf now. He is real for me. I have not experienced anything like this before. I took everything I could from him. Whether this was my incarnation or not I don't know, but I took everything I could. You need to do this to solve the assignment you need to solve.

*— I feel differently now. I feel free from fear not to have children now. As I listened to your story, I came to understand why I did not want to have children.*

— Let's take a broader look at what happened today. We started with Svetlana saying that she came to know her program and that she does not need anything anymore. And now it is being reinforced. You have said, "I am by myself. This is great. This is my program." Now we can better understand why this is the way it is.

*— Now I understand why I decided not to have children. I understand why I thought that it was painful, scary, and dangerous.*

157

*— This is a personal explanation. You, Svetlana, have a husband, and you don't have children. You are okay with that, even though I can see that you have a very strong maternal instinct. You realize it through your dogs and cats, but you will not give birth. You have not experienced pregnancy, and you have never delivered a baby.*

*— I will tell you more. I was pregnant when I was young, but I don't remember how many times. I forbid myself to remember that. I cannot say for sure how many abortions I had. As soon as I would get pregnant, I would have to get an abortion immediately. I would not even allow myself to think whether I wanted this baby or not. I would get rid of it as fast as I could.*

— Take a look at this well-known-to-everyone Pavlov's dog. Pavlov conducted experiments during which he explored behavioral reactions of dogs. There is a branch of psychology called behavioral psychology that uses his data. This is what man does to a dog. We are dealing with something similar here. Someone is studying a human being. What kind of an animal did we create, and what are its capabilities? Who is studying us? Those Nazis are just the performers. Who does it then?

*— The program gets reinforced when similar situations are experienced multiple times. The program's reaction should be instantaneous.*

— We have all read about extraterrestrials abducting people. Why do they do that? They do it because they have a problem with sexuality. They have been cloning themselves for a long time. They want to figure out what it is, and they have a very good playground here for this purpose. We are still quite sexual beings. They conduct their experiments and sometimes people disappear. People are being used by different civilizations for multiple purposes. We are dealing with a similar thing here. They experiment on us as we experiment on animals: how would a female animal that just gave birth react to her newborn baby being taken away from her?

158

*— I want to ask Dina something. You have said that you were a victim in that situation and you did not feel any pleasure.*

*— I did not feel pleasure there. In the previous incarnation, where I killed, I felt kaif from the killing itself.*

*— So, you were an oppressor and you experienced kaif from it. You are a victim here. And what do you feel?*

*— I have not deidentified yet.*

— Look deeper. You are both an oppressor and a victim there simultaneously. It is oppressing you, and you are a victim, but it is you who are the oppressor. It happens simultaneously. That's why you recalled this. This is your major theme. It should be investigated in detail. And to do that, you experience totally different incarnations. Your oppressor and your victim meet each other in this particular incarnation.

*— This topic got activated recently.*

*— My victim is in the "minus", and I am afraid to experience it.*

*— What does it mean for the victim to be in the "minus"? It's when you don't receive pleasure from being a victim. You are a victim, but you don't find it to be pleasant.*

## How does neutralization of a role occur?

— Every oppressor has a "plus" and a "minus". The same can be said about every victim. You can only get to know a role in a "plus" and in a "minus". That's the only way to neutralize a role. Neutralization occurs when you find "minus" in the "plus" and "plus" in the "minus". That's the only way to neutralize a role. In order to get to zero, you need to neutralize both sides.

*— I had a conflict with my neighbor, and my oppressor became active. If I were an oppressor in the "minus", I should also have a victim in the "minus", right?*

159

— You have said, "My victim is in the 'minus'." Okay. Now, you need to find the victim in the "plus". What you consider to be "minus" also gives you a "plus". This is that basic concept that we need to work through here. We work with perception. The world is the way you perceive it. We should not try to change the world; we should change our perception. To get to the level of free perception means to enter point zero. Otherwise, you are bound by your dual perception in the paradigm of duality. Our basic lesson here is to get out of the paradigm of duality. It is our perception of who should get out of it. You don't need to get rid of duality; your perception must exit to the zero point. You need to free your perception from duality.

Okay. Let's return to what you have said: "Victim is in the 'minus'". Tell me about this "minus" of yours. What kind of a "minus" is it?

— *I sublease a small bedroom in a two bedroom apartment that my friend rents. Her neighbor actually owns the place. He wants to evict me. He wants me out.*

— He does not want you to be there. He wants to throw you out.

— *Yes. Every time I pass him by, he reminds me that he is the landlord, and I am nobody.*

— And why do you think that you are the victim in this situation? Perhaps you are the oppressor? From his point of view, you are the oppressor. He is a victim of circumstances: someone he does not like moved into the apartment he owns. He feels that he is the victim. Can you see the situation from his point of view? Can you see that you are the oppressor here?

— *Yes. I prevent him from living peacefully.*

— Why don't you balance these two sides now? This guy needs this too. You have said that you prevent him from living peacefully. But he is bored with living peacefully. In order for him to understand that he wants to live with only one tenant, he needs you who would

160

prevent him from living with only one tenant. In that case, he can fight for the peaceful life with only one tenant. But he can only do this with you in the picture. He actually does not need this peaceful life. That's what we've been talking about all along. This is a drug.

— *And this is my drug, too. I use him and this conflict to feel life somehow.*

— You are doing it to feel that you are somebody. When he screams, he pays attention to you. Imagine, you are sitting in this studio of yours and no one looks at you, not even a mouse. You don't exist.

How do you know you are here? In order for you to know that, someone has to pay attention to you. What kind of attention is it? That's another question. He is paying you a lot of attention. You can feel your presence in this world. And he is the register that registers your existence.

— *We are involved in such a crazy fight!*

— Great! Now, look at the "plus" your ego receives out of it. "We have such a crazy fight!" You feel that you exist every day, and every day you feel it stronger and stronger!

— *I feel anger. I am angry at myself for repeating the same thing day after day.*

— Why are you angry at yourself for repeating the same thing? We eat every day and we use the bathroom every day. Are you angry at yourself for going to the bathroom every day?

— *I want us to have a truce, but I cannot bring him to partnership.*

— Wait a minute! Wait a minute! Let's not do this now, "I want to have truce." You are all such innocent saints. Take a look at what your ego receives: "I want to get attention, and I want them to acknowledge that I exist." This is the "plus".

You keep talking about the "minuses", but because of him you receive a constant, daily reaffirmation of your existence in this world. These reaffirmations are different. Someone reaffirms himself by saying, "Peter is sleeping with me. He is so good!" or "My boss is killing me! I keep arguing with him every day. I exist!" You found yourself a landlord who wants to kick you out—you exist! This is the basic moment for personality. If no one notices it, it does not exist. This is horrible.

Now look at your daily fights and problems and at the people you hate. They are the main evidence of your personal existence. You are acknowledged. How? What's the difference? Even love here gets extinguished fast. He kissed me ten times yesterday. Today he kissed me eight times. Tomorrow he will not even touch me. But your landlord keeps screaming! He is acknowledging you big time and nonstop!

— *It looks like one side wants this truce, but the other wants to fight.*

— Look. You need to know what the ego wants. You think, "Do I want the truce or not?" but the ego wants confirmation that it exists. Ego is an illusory construction. And what does the illusory construction want? It wants to have proofs that it exists. As soon as these proofs disappear, it disappears with them. That's why it needs to confirm the fact of its existence. So, what do I tell you? These so-called positive or "plus" confirmations—petting and kissing—are short-lived. What's basic here is irritation, anger, hatred, and wrath, which grow fast. And ego receives what it needs, i.e. confirmation of its existence.

— *So one needs to see and connect it.*

— Wait a minute! Do not hurry! Try to process what I have just said. That's not what you were thinking a minute ago. Anna was saying she wanted to come to some kind of a truce. It's not pleasant when someone screams and yells at you. And, in reality, her neighbor is equally irritated. He is very irritated! And why did you, Anna, get stuck in this? There are other neighbors, quiet neighbors. You might have gotten yourself a comatose neighbor. Hmmm? Look, you are living next to your man.

— *Yes. My dad and my son are my copies. I realized recently that they are my copies.*

— Your parts keep telling you, "You exist, Anny! We are your parts?" And they scream and scream.

— *You have sorted this topic very well with me during the last webinar. I understand now that I was demanding confirmation of my existence from every boyfriend of mine. He was supposed to call me all the time: "You are my girlfriend. You exist. I need you." That was mandatory. And how does it manifest itself now? I went to a party with my new boyfriend. We came home, and I started nagging him: "I did not like your behavior there. It appeared as if we were not a couple." And I catch myself feeling as if I was not there. If I don't receive a confirmation, my personality gets lost immediately.*

— *I just realized that my affinity to the glamorous life is the way for my ego to confirm its existence. If I am well-dressed and have money in my pocket—I exist.*

— It's clear to everyone that there are diamonds around, but what's of major importance is the fact that they are mine.

— *Yes, the more dresses and Gucci bags I have in my closet, the more I exist.*

— Yes. One must tie oneself to what exists. What is fashionable definitely exists, and if I am dressed in fashionable clothes, I exist. This is the essence of the phenomena. Fashion changes fast, and if I am still wearing this skirt, it means I don't exist, because other skirts are fashionable this season.

— *That's why she has dresses falling out of her closet, and she cannot decide what to wear.*

— *Svetlana has to live another side of life. Bring it all here and give it away.*

— *I felt freer just thinking that I could get rid of it.*

*— You just flipped. Wait a minute and you will recall, "One sable coat. One mink coat."*

— And under item twenty-eight, "Get lost all of you! I exist!" And you go, and you buy another coat. **So, what does it mean to come to the Real Owner? It means the old one should step down. But as long as he is important and insists that he exists, he will not recognize any other owners at all. This is what it means to come to zero. This is a state of "I don't exist."** Can you even experience that? But this is precisely the moment that will bring you to what and who you really are. Currently, you are taking fiction to be you. This is fiction. "Do I exist or not?" is a question everyone asks from time to time.

And now take a look at the era of total control we have entered. Everything you say is being recorded. You can be found anywhere around the globe almost instantly. There is a talk about chips being implanted into our bodies. We are going to resemble completely identifiable cars. It sounds horrible, but that is what the ego needs. "I exist. What they do to me is painful, but I exist."

So, the question is to be or to have? The path of the ego is through "to have". The more it has, there more it exists. This is the key question of a human being: "I am nobody. I am shit." And then we flip: "I am everything!" Let's sort it out. What does "everything" mean? Everything is actually God that has not been manifested. And what are we? We are something concrete. And the concrete ego is identified with its concreteness, doubts it constantly, and get nervous and excited over it all the time. It cannot understand that it is everything. You consider yourself to be somebody, but the opposite side is: you can never understand that you are everything. Only when you come to understand that you are everything will you be able to become someone. We have arrived at a very interesting question. How does ego see the fact of its existence?

164

*— It was given a physical body, but it still does not believe.*

— The physical body is temporary. The basic fear people have is "What will happen after death?" They find the idea of parting with the physical body horrible. They sit at funerals crying and screaming, "Why did you leave us?" Who was there? Who was this man who spent all this time in this physical body?

Try to imagine what we are discussing here. Imagine that we are one. Imagine we never part. Imagine there is no death. This image may pacify you somewhat, but it's incomprehensible. How can we be "one", and at the same time there are many of us? And where would we return to? We would return into this "one". It means we don't part. We part when we leave this "oneness" and separate from it. For some reason, we cry when the transfer back home occurs. That means we consider this "one" to be somewhat abstract.

*— But these rules, the rules that we don't remember, who we are and what is going to happen after death, were created for a reason. Were they not?*

— Yes, that's what this reality was created for. It was created in order for a human being to obtain this experience. The state of conflict can only be experienced in a state of total forgetfulness. And as I said before, the basic guilt of a human being, which later on separates into different forms, originates from forgetfulness. This is guilt of the ego that rejected God, i.e. what it really is, imagining yourself to be the owner.

# The Process of one's Transformation and Resurrection

*— Then what's all of this for?*

— The question deals with the acquisition of necessary energies. As we have already discussed, suffering represents the type of energy that we are receiving here. We are here to receive this experience and to investigate this reality. When miners descend into a mine, they don't think "Why am I here? Who thought up this coal? What is this mine for?" No. They start to dig. Our task is similar. We must dive deep into the dense vibrations.

This energy is very important and necessary. That's why our Supreme Aspects respect us. The Supreme Aspects are parts of God, and they send us, their own parts, here. It is not coincidental that Jesus is the son of God. God sent his own son here. He did not send someone else. We are the sons and daughters of God. We need to find Jesus inside ourselves.

For centuries, it was presented differently. Jesus was God's son, and the rest of us were sinners. This is not the case anymore. You will have to find Jesus inside yourself. You will have to look and find God inside yourself. People search in the wrong places. They have gotten lost inside, but they search outside.

— *I used to come home from the seminar before radiating energy. But this time it is different. I come home, and I cannot recall what we talked about here. My personality has closed up completely.*

— Do not consider something to be closed or open. This is just your explanation. Remain in these states and experience them to the fullest. What must be born will be born in these states. You want to recreate something. That's how it was back then. Today it is different. You will be given what you need, and every time it will be different. Do not apply explanations to it. Do not apply past situations to it. We need to be present to the states we are currently in, and we need to extract what we need to extract from them. This is what entering the unknown is about. You experienced something back then, and now you experience something else. Enter what you are supposed to enter without judgment and extract what you need to extract. What is it? You don't even know. You will be able to receive it only when you have experienced it.

— *My personality looks at Zoey crying and Dina talking through her pain, and it keeps thinking, "Where is your pain? Where is it?"*

— Do not compare yourself to others.

— *While listening to the last webinar, I realized that I am just a small screw. I have only one choice. I must keep going. Personality has two options. It can participate in the Process and everything is going to be all right, or it can resist and go the other way. In that case, it will be destroyed. In essence, it does not have a choice. But this is not a hopeless situation. We are all interconnected here. When one of us solves something, it reflects on every one of us. This cannot be understood on the physical level. When one returns to this game and resumes the fight, one cannot see it.*

— And take a look at the transformations. How does the Phoenix get reborn? Self-resurrection is the main thing here. I know this very well based on my own experience. The personality is very self-important initially. Suddenly, it flips into "I am nothing. I am just a program. I am just a tiny screw in a big machine." This is the duality personality fluctuates in: "I am very important—I am nothing." You must get to the point zero. That's when the relationship of the Supreme Aspect to the lower aspect will change.

We can spend hours talking about it, but you need to experience this and find it inside yourself. My Supreme Aspect has a great respect for my lower aspect, and my lower aspect has a great respect for my Supreme Aspect. They respect each other equally. But this did not happen right away. This transformation took a long time. You need to pass these stages. You need to pass the stage of the personality, which appraises the fact of its existence. That's the experience you acquire when you are being screamed and yelled at, i.e. "I exist".

You will not be able to understand what I say about the lower and the Supreme Aspect until your personality has undergone a

167

transformation. Ego should transform these energies and become the lower aspect. Lowest does not mean bad. Otherwise, the way it is now, it is just ego, personality. That's what it is. You don't call yourself lower aspect, right? "Who are you?" — "I am Svetlana, the lower aspect."

— *I can tell you one thing, I feel all of us. We are small and isolated parts, but we are one.*

— That's right. We already experience this "WE".

# Gratitude to father and mother is the door to the Supreme Aspect

— *I want to say something about this interaction between my Supreme Aspect and my lower aspect. Some time ago, my personality accepted that there is something out there that is higher than it, and that this "Higher" has its own intention. It was very painful for my personality, and it tried to resist. But at a certain point, I came to understand that this is how it is going to be. And personality surrendered. I realize now that this was acceptance of the True Owner.*

— This was a true surrender. We've talked about it a lot.

— *Yes. Surrender. I entered a key situation of my life in a reverse order last night. It turns out that the story I told you is not primary. It's a consequence of what happened in childhood. I saw yesterday that this show was the exact replica of the show that was played out during my parents' divorce. The wife—the lover— the father—and the child who observes it all. The plot is the same.*

*My mother is not giving my dad any feelings. Her work is very important for her and she does not care for him. Father is searching for feelings and finds another woman. It appears that this woman gives him feelings, but in reality, she asserts her own importance by snatching an important man from a rich business woman. This woman was of a very low social status, but she was able to outwit my Mom. Father is initially torn between the duty with which Mom oppresses him and the feelings that another woman offers him. Finally, he chooses feelings and leaves, rejecting this debt.*

*There is something very interesting here. The child observes all of this, and at some point, this little girl makes a choice. She chooses her dad. She chooses feelings and remains true to these feelings. She is condemned for that by her mother and learns to hide her feelings. She learns to hide them very well. For the rest of her life, she will be afraid that Mom and other people will discover that, in reality, she loves her dad. She is morbidly afraid to be found out, and she hides these feelings masterfully. And the same show will be played out twenty years later with two men. But this now all-grown-up adolescent girl initially also chooses feelings, but she cannot follow them, and she chooses duty. She experiences duty. And it seems to me that it is precisely at this moment that she starts to reject her father. She betrays father, and the conflict she experienced with Mom prior to that moment resolves.*

*After experiencing this situation, rejecting feelings and choosing duty, she flips. By rejecting her father, she accepts Mom. I was crying on the way here, but suddenly I saw all of this as a show. I saw every actor of this show differently. I don't blame any one of them. I understand them all. I returned to this situation yesterday, and I allowed myself to experience what each one of them had experienced. I felt this interaction between the Higher and the lower aspects. It seems to me that the one who observes all of this accepts the lower aspect. Yes, this is my lower aspect, with all these games, betrayals, and suffering. But I understand now that this is a show.*

— I can tell you more. Your Higher Aspect applauds you for an amazing performance.

— *I don't hear these applauds, and I don't feel them.*

— Not yet. Not yet.

— *I understand that applauds will end this game. Why don't I hear them now?*

— Because the show is not finished yet.

169

*— I still don't understand what kind of an assignment it was. Perhaps I have to connect duty and feelings.*

**— You have to connect Mom and Dad. This connection is a door to the Supreme Aspect. Gratitude. When you start to feel this gratitude, you will hear applause, and flowers will be thrown to your feet.**

*— I applaud you, Zoey. I am grateful to you for sharing this story. This is also my story. I've experienced it, too. I've been through the same show with my parents and my men. Thank you for allowing me to see it so clearly.*

— Take a close look at Zoey. She experiences things, and she can clearly describe what she experienced later on.

*— I want to express my gratitude too. I have observed how difficult and painful it was for you to re-live all of this. It was a hard work. As you were describing your situation, I was reliving my own story. You've made my work easier. You have mentioned the need to connect duty and feelings, and I suddenly saw that I need to accept my father leaving us. And I have to accept my husband's recurrent travels. I have to accept it with gratitude.*

*— I noticed quite a few similarities between my story and Zoey's story, too. I loved my dad dearly, but I had to hide it, too. I can express love to my mother, but I am forbidden to express love to my dad. That's where fear comes from. I am afraid she will discover this betrayal of mine. I have always felt guilty around my dad. I have always felt this hypocrisy. Eventually, I got very tired of it. I started to blame him for drinking, and I felt better. I found a way to condemn him and to not feel guilty. So, guilt flipped into condemnation, but the fear remains. I am constantly afraid of my plot being discovered. This is my drug.*

*— I have experienced enormous gratitude to my dad, too. He has played his role well. He did everything so my sister and I would hate him. He did everything for us to blame him. He drank and smoked. He could allow himself a tantrum. He would intensify it to make it easier for us. He played his role so well that it was easy for us to condemn him.*

170

— Imagine you have two saints in your life—Mom and Dad. What will your life look like? It will be horrible. But if one of them is nasty, everything works great.

— *A couple years ago, I finally saw why dad had to start drinking. Why did he have to look for another woman and feelings on the side? He had to do it because Mom would not let him have it at home. She never did. She still does not give anything to him. And he hits his head on the wall, unable to figure out what exactly he misses. He needs feelings, but she would not give him any. I grew up exactly like her.*

— *My parents lived separately. I don't know how it happened. When Dad would stop by, everything would go amok. Mom would break dishes and curse him. He lives, and I think to myself, "Thank God! Dad left!" After a while I would miss him. I was always ambivalent. I wanted him to come, but at the same time, I didn't want him to come. Who did that? That was Mom. She would create such strong tension that he would leave after fifteen minutes of being there.*

*My older brothers would dangle a candy in front of me. I would follow them into a dark room, and they would lock me in there. Candy has meant something else for me ever since. Candy is a treat I get after I experience a dangerous situation. It is always followed by self blame.*

— Candy for you is what cheese in a mouse trap is for a mouse.

— *The fact that older brothers were fooling me got fixed in me. It was bad. Older is bad. Older man is bad. When my brother killed his friend, kids started to call me "killer's sister". I used to blame myself for being a killer's sister.*

— Ah, these damned men. It's a paradox, but Pint is a man, and he tells us about the Supreme Aspect. Can something good come from a man? Is he going to fool us using a candy called the Supreme Aspect?

— *I have experienced that, too: "Pint doesn't understand me. He constantly interrupts me."*

— If he were to understand me, he would listen to me for hours.

171

*— Yes, I understand that this is my external projection: "I don't understand. I don't listen."*

*— It's totally opposite in my case. I don't like men, but at the same time, I am very masculine. I also did not like the way adults behaved, but I wanted to grow up fast.*

# Acceptance of the paternal and maternal programs, and experiencing their fight

**— That is what it means to learn "from the opposite". "He is nasty" — you say, not noticing that you behave exactly the same way. You don't see it, but this is how it is being absorbed. It's precisely through dislike that you copy every quality of a human being who causes you to experience this dislike. In fighting your enemy, you turn into your enemy.**

*— That's how we come to know the opposite part.*

*— I got to know this by fighting my neighboor. I realized that he was me.*

— "You will find your enemy in the fight," the old song goes. Until you get to know and become aware that your enemy is you, you will continue to fight.

*— I got it. I accept my mom's program. That's why I have such a good relationship with my daughter.*

— This is what ancestral programs are all about. When you reject your father, you are in the mother role. When you reject your mother, you are in the father.

*— This is how Anna creates this reality. She creates a certain situation where, for example, her husband blames her for something. And she starts to judge herself, "I am so bad!" This happens all the time. I do something. He reacts this way, and I consider myself guilty.*

— My program was built in a very interesting way. I have accepted the role of the mother. Women who accept the role of the mother can get together and chastise men. Men who accept the role of the father can get together and chastise women. In my case, it is completely screwed up. I have blamed myself for being a man. That led me to open up the Matrix.

— *How can that be? I accepted my dad's program. So, why do I dislike men? And yet at the same time, it is much easier for me to communicate and deal with men.*

— Do you consider yourself to be a man?

— *No, of course, not.*

— Okay. In that case, you do not experience pain for hurting men. I, on the other hand, while being a man and having strongly-expressed masculine qualities, always blamed myself for inflicting pain on men. Your case is different. You consider yourself to be a woman. If you were to consider yourself to be a man, you would experience the pain you inflict on men. For example, you stood him up, and you feel his pain.

— *In my case it is different. It is irrelevant to me whether it is a man who is hurting or a woman. Whenever someone feels bad, I feel bad.*

— This is a heightened perception. **I am showing you different types of perceptions. When I was in elementary school, we had a motto, "You are good, and I am good." But my program was different, "You feel bad, and I feel bad." I could not feel good when someone felt bad. Even now, as long as you feel bad, I cannot feel good. So, I am interested in you feeling good.**

— *Every one of us came to School because of pain. Every one of us wants to get rid of it.*

— Hang yourself or go to School.

173

— *Yes. And now we are not hurting that much, and we feel somewhat strange. Where is our pain? It looks like we forgot why we came. Everything is being slowly balanced.*

— *Moreover, personality starts to create very interesting situations. I don't even have time for self-investigation anymore.*

— As soon as the level of pain diminishes, personality becomes active. As soon as you feel bad, you run to Pint.

— *Should I investigate my dad's program through a man?*

— This is a good question. Things frequently get flipped here. It is common for a father to carry emotional states. When that happens, a mom accepts the role of a man.

— *My mother is pure emotion. I don't know my dad at all.*

— It means his predominant center was the intellectual center.

— *Mom used to hurt me emotionally. She would hurt her men emotionally, too.*

— The fact that you don't remember your dad doesn't mean he doesn't exist. We are dealing with energies here. This energy will come to you dressed differently. That's a fact, and I am pretty sure you have already encounter that. You had to.

— *My understanding of my dad occurs through mom's perception. She transmits that in her stories and in her attitude toward my dad. This is how and what is absorbed.*

— Yes. Dad is also always present through Mom, through what Mom used to say about him.

— *You have experienced a very strong imprint: "He does not exist!" You were brought to the door, and you were asked to knock on it. Mom did everything she could for you to remember your father in this situation. She did everything she could so that you would hate him.*

— This part of the program perceives through hate. What happens next? What quality are we dealing with? **From the metaphysical point of view, a man stands for the mind, while a**

174

woman represents feelings. We usually see ourselves from the point of view of the physical body alone, but as we can see now, quite frequently the feminine program works in a man, while the masculine program works in a woman. In essence, feminism is about a war between men in women's bodies against men in men's bodies.

— *Thank you. I just realized that I carry Dad's program on the conscious level. My dad was a cold, unemotional guy with a highly developed intellect. From the early days, it was forbidden for me to manifest feelings. To manifest feelings was equal to admitting one's weakness in our family. You could not do it, because it is the strongest who survives in the world of survival. Feelings are weakness. Eventually, Dad committed suicide by sticking a knife in his own heart. This was his last attempt to open his heart.*

— This was his last attempt to close his heart. He was fighting his heart all his life, and he manifested it physically. He had a difficult program.

— *I can clearly see that I follow his footsteps. I don't feel anything. I don't manifest any feelings. It is forbidden to me.*

— Yes. You know how it ends.

— *But you came here in the feminine body. It means you have more chances to find and manifest your feelings.*

— *He used to condemn himself for manifesting feelings, and he condemned others for it. I have never seen him cry. He did not even cry when his mother died.*

— *But if I remember correctly, you mentioned he was also on a spiritual search.*

— *Yes. But this was a mental search. He used to read the Bible and underline every line there, but it was an intellectual pursuit. He did not feel anything.*

— The basic question of philosophy is, "How to commit a proper suicide?"

*— Yes, I found a pack of notes after his death. He contemplated different ways to leave this world.*

— This is the basic question of philosophy, "How to commit a proper suicide?" The basic question religion asks is, "Do I believe or not?"

*— He wanted to come to know how things are on the other side.*

— And he decided to get to know this faster. Take a look at any theater show. What do actors bring to a show when they play it? They bring their feelings into it. It's one thing to read a script of a show monotonously, and a totally different thing to read it with feelings. We are dealing with the same thing here. It seems to some of us that they come here to learn something, and they search for the Truth. This is the pursuit of philosophy. What is the Truth? We come here to obtain a certain experience, but they search for the intellectual Truth. They can't find it, and they will never find it. And eventually, many philosophers face this question: "I did not find what I was searching for. How do I die now?"

**We come here to acquire a certain experience, i.e. feelings. You have closed the door on the basics. The script will come alive when you start to feel and experience it. You are just reading it now. You have been reading it your whole life. Start to feel it. Start to experience it.**

## The real transformation occurs through a change in perception

*— If I understand you correctly, the inner states cannot be described mentally. One can only experience them. My intellectual center constantly tries to describe what I experience using words.*

— Let's take a look at what you brought up using a theater analogy, where five actresses want to play the role of Juliet. They come to an audition where a director asks them to perform a certain part of the script. They do that. Each one of them goes through the same lines. But each one of them brings totally different feelings to the stage. One of them just stands there speaking her lines monotonously. Another speaks the same lines, but she appears anxious and animated. The same play, staged by different directors and played by different actors, can be seen totally differently.

Take Chekov's *Seagull* for example. It has been staged many times, but every time it is different. It depends on the actors who participate in the play and what they invest in their performance. The experience, however, is limited by the script, i.e. there is a certain text and a certain context that the actor should follow. These give birth to different feelings, as we can see.

So, the program represents a certain script. The scenes of your script will repeat themselves and recur. But if you transform, you will experience them differently, even though the context will be the same. The show continues, but as you start to change, you play your role differently.

**Take the death of a loved one, for example. It's a horrible nightmare for you. You cry your eyes out. Another death—you cry again. Another death—you cry again. The fourth death. Suddenly, you start to experience death differently. Did your program change? No. You've changed. Your perception has changed. The scenario is the same, but your perception has changed. We don't change the scenario. We change our perceptions.**

**Everyone here tries to change the external world but to no avail. You need to change your perception. That will lead to**

**true transformation. This is what true spirituality is about. Spirituality is in the mastery of perception.**

Imagine a scene. A woman comes forward and starts to accuse a man for leaving her. "Bastard! How could you leave me?! How could you betray me?!" Or she might say, "Thank you. I was waiting for you to do that for a long time." Or, "How do you like it there? Does she cook well? Does she take care of you?" Take a look at how differently one scene can be played out. It's a totally different perception. Do I perceive him as an enemy who betrayed me or as someone who is having a difficult time?

— *Something happened to me in childhood that I still cannot sort out. I have fooled myself. How do I experience this situation? I feel bad. I cry. Mentally, I am grateful to this man for what he did for me. He left because our relationship had ended. But my emotions can't process it. I continue to blame and hate him. I can come and say, "Thank you dear for what you've done." I still feel this aggression inside me.*

— If you do that, you will face the incongruence between your words and the states you experience. It's one thing when you feel that he is a bastard and you tell him that, and it is a different thing when you feel that he is a bastard and thank him for what he has done. Your head understands one thing, but your heart feels something else. **The first step that you need to make in order to change your perception is to do what you feel.** You need to experience this hatred and aggression. Until you allow yourself to experience it in full, you will be stuck in one place; you will not be able to move forward.

— *But I can't scream at home and throw dishes around.*

— You can't do that because you consider the mind to be the master. You think that if you came to understand that everything was done correctly, and everything is good, you would express gratitude to him. But this is not what your heart feels. You must accept that your heart is the main director, and you should come from the heart. And if you have anger and hatred there, you must verbalize and express it. Otherwise, you are putting your foot on a break, and will bring yourself to an inner dissonance when you say one thing but feel something totally different. Allow yourself to experience and to verbalize what you feel. Otherwise, your emotional center is being suppressed by your intellectual center.

— *I keep telling him that I wish him happiness, but he is convinced I hate him.*

— When you say that now, I feel it. A child catches the feelings, not the words. I frequently use profanities, but you feel tenderness behind my words. Someone who is not familiar with what we do here may get confused hearing these words, but I show you that even profanities can express tenderness.

— *I listened to your audio recording once, where a woman accused you of using foul language, and you replied to her that she can't hear anything aside from that. It was so funny.*

— *Uri, who is usually very quiet, has been screaming at me for the past few days. When I asked him why, he said that this was the only way for him to shut me up and make me listen to what he has to say.*

— *Can I ask you a question? I have started to think about my parents. Based on my program, I also reject my father. He was a professional sailor, and he would spend most of his time on the boat. When he would come home, he would be drunk most of the time. Mom always positioned herself as a lone saint: "I have to do everything while he is having his fun at sea. Then he comes home, and he has fun here, too. Everything is on my shoulders."*

*I have accepted her program with a harsh mental center. I got married, and here is something I cannot figure out. I started to fight with my husband right away. I have cried day and night. What was this? Was my emotional center overriding my intellectual center?*

— What did you fight over? Did you fight over him not making enough money?

— *We had various conflicts. As a child, I got used to the fact that when Dad was home, we would spend this time partying and meeting his friends. That was normal for me. He used to say, "Five minutes to be ready!" and I was ready. But when I got married, I flipped into a role of a wife. I had to stay home with my husband watching TV. This was a shock.*

— This is your mom's dream. Her husband was out sailing all the time. You are dealing with the opposite side. Your husband is home all the time. You need to come to know the opposite side.

— *I tried to get out of the house all the time. Any excuse I could find, I would be out. And at the same time, I felt guilty around my husband for leaving him alone.*

— In doing that, you behave like your father, while your husband performs the opposite side by sitting at home—no sea and no party. Home and only home. This is the opposite side. You need to see this side and accept it.

— *I behaved the way my father did, while my husband behaved like my mom.*

— Okay. If you think that's the case, you need to see exactly what this side manifested itself in. We need to have very clear analogies. What did your mom demand from your dad, and what did your husband demand of you? These demands should be similar. You are never home. You are partying all the time. He is mirroring to you the maternal part of the program, while you are in the paternal part of the program.

— *Hmmm, I have always condemned my husband for not making enough money.*

— Okay. What does that mean? It means we are dealing with a combination here: you are father one day, and mother the next day. This must be discerned very accurately.

— *Wow. This is very interesting. Can the program of the stepfather work here, too?*

— *Do foster parents introduce their programs in us, too?*

— Of course, they do.

# CHAPTER 5
# THE EMOTIONAL AND PHYSICAL EXPERIENCE OF THE STATES "OPPRESSOR—VICTIM"

•◆•◆•◆•◆•◆•◆•◆•◆•◆•◆•◆•◆•◆•◆•◆•◆•◆•◆•◆•◆•◆•◆•

## How do you sense the seminar?

*— I said yesterday that I have a sensation that nothing is happening. Actually, this is not what I feel. I understand that something is happening, but I don't have any clear thoughts in my head. I don't have a clear understanding of what's going on. My head is empty and clean. I don't feel anything. I don't feel any emotions. My physical body was hurting yesterday. I think everything was dropped to the physical level, bypassing the mental and intellectual centers.*

— Great! Your sensations from Pint's seminar are, "My joints were hurting" or, "It was a great seminar. I came home with a headache."

*— My head is spinning. I was thinking about the narcotic states we discussed yesterday. It looks like I recently got dependent on the fluctuation in the states of my "Victim—Oppressor" duality.*

— And you can't think about anything because your joints are hurting.

*— Yes. It is difficult for me to think.*

— Everyone is sad, and we are all looking at Natalie while experiencing our own heartburn. Now we can all appraise the happiness of our forgetting ourselves, the happiness of sleep.

*— This morning I was thinking about how each one of us creates hell in his life and lives happily there. We only notice this hell when we are being pulled into*

*some other kind of life. For some reason, I only notice it during the seminars. I have the feeling I want to live anywhere but home. My girlfriend visited me, and she expressed the same thought: "It's so good here. I don't want to go home." Every one of us has been so washed out in what he has created that we don't even notice the place where we live. For us, it is just a place. We are not happy with the city we live in. We are not happy with the house we live in. But if we were to move somewhere else, we would create the same thing we have created here. That's what I saw today.*

— It's a dead end. It turns out you cannot get away from it. As I said before, it is hard to get out of it. The first round was not successful. We are stuck in the depressive dead end of hopelessness. Let's go for another round.

— *I feel that some deep work is being done now. Something is happening, but it is not clear to me what it is exactly. Let's try to bring it to the mental level. Otherwise, it is a dead-end.*

— *Lately, in connection with my disease, I have been rejecting the mode of survival. First of all, I feel that I don't have the energy for it. I don't have any energy to invest in the modes of survival I know, and as a result, there is no desire either. I understand that I was flipped from the mode of survival into the opposite side. I got interested in this, and I started to think about it in order to collect all of this into a whole picture. After a while, I started to feel happy… I have stopped seeing meaning in survival, but today I clearly saw how important survival is for walking the Path we are walking. It offers me the material means to support myself.*

— Don't forget that your ability to survive also supports Pint, to whom you pay money to keep Holistic Psychology alive. That should make all of you happier.

— *I have experienced total rejection of the material world.*

— And the material world started to reject you. You are pushing each other.

*— It is very important not to push each other here, but to understand who needs who and why. Spiritual evolution brings a certain meaning to the material world. Eventually, being totally submerged into the material world, one starts to understand that he is going to boil in the same thing for the rest of his life. One starts to realize that this is the dead end.*

*— Today, speaking through my friend, I have said to myself, "I feel so bad! I am short of money again!" As I was saying it to her, I understood that I was saying it to myself. "Perhaps, it is time to start working on the spiritual side of me." When one gets stuck in the material dead end, one should pull up the second side of duality. That will allow me to go forward.*

— Great! Now, you have a thought in your head, "I don't have the money." It's a great thought. It elevates your body temperature. It gives your muscles energy.

## "The victim is also the oppressor at the same time"

*— Can I say something? Yesterday, I tried to sort out how my depression started. I saw that the same situation keeps reoccurring again and again. It is some kind of punishment, but I cannot sort out why I am being punished. Someone does something to me, and I expect a totally different reaction. I don't even understand why it is being done. I don't even need to feel guilty. No one accuses me of anything.*

*For example, when I came to Tbilisi with my husband, his mom did not want to meet me. She was against our marriage. She tried to prevent it any way she could. I did not understand it. "Why? What did I do to you? Let's get to know each other." All my attempts were unsuccessful. And the same thing happens in school. I am a good student, and I get good grades, but very soon I get attached to something else. I have experienced this again and again. I have been experiencing this in Tbilisi all the time. And then I got depressed. Finally, I understood that I do not allow myself to manifest aggression. I have read many smart books, and I have tried to do what many of them recommended, i.e. to accept and to come to love everyone. In reality, I am ready to kill everyone now.*

— So, why don't you allow yourself to do that? Why don't you allow yourself to kill everyone around you?

— *I could not even say anything to my parents-in-law.*

— Why don't you send them a postcard: "Happy birthday. I'll come over tonight and kill you both."

— *When someone is rude to me on the bus, I can't even say something back. I can't say, "Shut up, you idiot!" These words don't come out of my mouth. I kept thinking all last night, "Why can't I say that?"*

— That's a good question. Why can't you?

— *It started during early childhood. First of all, my mom is not adequate in her reactions sometimes. I could have been doing something good, but she would come and yell at me.*

— You think that if you are good or doing something good, you cannot be insulted. But it turns out, this is not the case. It can be quite the opposite.

— *Aside from this, I have a "very good" brother who is ten years my senior. He used to beat the hell out of me when I was young. When he got married, he started to beat his wife. He would beat me for no reason.*

— What do you mean, for no reason? You are a woman! He could have killed you for this reason alone. He was getting his training with you, and when he got married, he was ready to give his wife a really good beating.

— *I remember this sate very well. No one was doing anything. Mom would say a few words to him for appearances sake. Dad did not even see it from his couch.*

— You are a girl for the beating.

185

*— Yes. That's who I am. I cannot say anything. I am afraid to talk to him. I am afraid to be in one room with him. I say a wrong word, and he starts to kick me.*

*— Even now?*

*— No, not now. I don't see much of him now. I don't think he would do anything bad now, but I am scared nevertheless.*

— Take a look at this. You are a professional victim. You express fear. The oppressor feels it and runs toward you. You express more fear, and he gets crazy. You must start to express your inner oppressor. You have not been taught to do that. Let us teach you. Okay. I want you to feel out a victim here. Take a look around. There are victims here.

*— Natalie or Irina. Who wants to be the victim?*

— Don't ask them. You are the oppressor now. You decide. You can hit both of them. Do it. You need an idea. What can you hate them for?

*— Do you hate men?*

*— Not only men. I hate everyone: Mom, Dad, my brother...*

— You have this global hatred inside. Ideology does not support your hatred. Normally, according to commonly accepted ideology, a child should respect his or her parents. Poor workers existed for centuries until Karl Marx offered them a proper ideology. And look what they did! You need to have some kind of ideology.

*— I want to tell you that when you were crying and I was playing your mom, I felt that you were playing the victim, but your victim oppresses others very well.*

— You have to feel this oppressor inside of you. You have a very good, strong oppressor inside.

*— I don't understand. I am very irritated now. Why are you hitting me? I am so small. I was expecting you to take care of me, but you are hurting me. You need to use your head.*

*— I don't want to use my head. I am going to kick you again now.*

186

*— Don't you think I can kick you back?*

*— Try it!*

— Okay. Imagine that. You are not just a little girl. You represent the whole Soviet Union. Here is Hitler. Keep this idea in mind. You have the idea that you are a little girl who no one should touch. But who can we touch if not you?

*— Why are you crying? You can't even hit me back! Try to hit me!*

— This is the first round. Seven hundred thirty-five fights are behind Alina's back, but she did not win even one of them. Look around you. There are women here who have husbands, lovers, and kids. Take a good look at them. These women can have husbands and lovers at the same time. This is real life, not your "sort of a life".

*— I don't need a lover. I don't need him at all. I want to lead a nice, quiet life.*

*— I don't need love. Just don't hurt me.*

*— I have love in my life.*

— What kind of love is it without a good beating? Don't you remember the old Russian proverb, "If he beats you, he loves you."

*— That's why you have "sort of a husband".*

*— I have a normal husband!*

*— C'mon!*

— Don't try to fool these women.

*— Women don't like it when someone has a normal husband and a normal relationship at twenty-four.*

*— This is not a fact. Who knows whether you have a normal husband or not.*

— Exactly. And whether you even have a husband. Are these children you keep talking about really yours?

*— Do you think that if I am the youngest here that I don't understand anything? Why do you think I cannot love? Why do you think my husband was "sort of a husband"? Why? Do you think I came here for nothing? All my friends*

*are clubbing, but I am bored with night life. I am here. Do you think I came here to be entertained? Perhaps you will give me some credit? Perhaps you will get it through your heads that I understand something?*

— I will tell you something more: "You understand more than all of them combined. They only think of money and lovers."

*— You say what you feel while we forgot everything a long time ago.*

*— Why are you so agressive?*

— Go ahead. Take it all out on them! Give it to them now! Let them know who is a woman here.

*— I did not have a husband when I was twenty-four. I did not think of anything at that age.*

*— When I was twenty-four, I had a husband and three kids.*

*— When I was twenty-four, I had two kids but I didn't have a husband.*

— Take a look at the difficult lives they had. Of course, they don't understand anything. Tell them, Alina! Tell them everything the way it is.

*— I used to kick and hurt my younger sister, too. I understand why I did it. My parents loved her more. She was younger. She was very quiet and positive, while I was a tomboy. When we did something good, my parents always praised her. When we did something bad, I was always the one to blame.*

## Transfer from a state of a victim into a state of an oppressor and back

— I have told you upfront that she is a "professional victim". How do you think oppressors get attracted to their victims? We got used to the concept of "innocent victim" here. This is not true. There are no innocent victims here. It is precisely the victim who attracts the oppressor. This happens on the energy level. Every victim releases energy of a certain quality to which aggressors react. The

188

external reasons are of little relevance here. You are attracting them energetically. Do you understand? But in this case, you need to get to know the opposite side of this duality. Your oppressor is equally powerful. You cannot move into your oppressor. You have a prohibition to do that! Most likely, you have played this role too many times in other lives.

— *Can I play a victim? I need to do that.*

— Why don't you stand accross from each other and start. Don't just kick each other. You have to feel it thoroughly. Our goal is not to hurt or kill each other. You need to feel your oppressor. Hit her and feel it. You have to feel what you feel and what she feels at the same time. Feel it thoroughly. You are afraid to hit her, but you need to pass this threshold and talk about it. Talk about what you feel.

— *My whole structure protests against this. I don't want to hit her!*

— Keep talking until something else comes up. Keep talking about your states.

— *When I hit her, I feel as though I am hitting myself.*

— Exactly. But you must get into your oppressor and experience pleasure from hitting her. You have to feel it. You are hitting yourself, but now you are in the oppressor. Oppressors feel pleasure in hitting other people. Recall how your brother did it. Do it! Keep talking. What's going on? Did your state change?

— *Yes, I am in a different state now.*

— Keep going. Do you feel good now? You feel good! Can you feel it? Do you feel how good your brother felt kicking you? Do you feel this energy? Hit her and say it. Imagine you are kicking your brother! Keep talking.

— *You are such a bastard! You keep hurting me because I cannot give it back to you. Do you think I can't kick you back? Here you go! How do you like this?*

189

— You are not a helpless Alina now. Do you feel this energy inside your body? Do you want to kick somebody else?

— *Yes!*

— What does the oppressor feel? "You are such a chicken! You are so weak. How can I not kick you?!" And he gets all puffed up. He feels great. She cannot do anything to him. How do you feel? Do you feel good?

— *I feel good.*

— *Anna, you wanted to experience the victim's "minus", but you are having kaif.*

— That's good. Let her experience the victim's "plus". Go ahead. Do you want to kick a couple more of these creeps? Look at them... Let them tremble!

— *You know, Anna, I am afraid of you now.*

— Here you go. She moved to a different state. They are feeling afraid of you.

— *I feel this energy, and I want to kick them, too.*

— Okay. Let's work with you now. One of you hits another. Then you reverse the roles. You are in a great state, Alina. You are in a fighter state. Hey, you! Don't you dare to defend yourself now. Stop! What state are you in?

— *I feel physical pain now, but I also feel excited.*

— *I feel that something is coming from me.*

— Become aware of everything, and keep talking.

— *I started to feel pity.*

— Pity?! The oppressor should not be pitied.

— *You get hit, and you immediately recall the victim.*

— Look. It turns out that when you feel pity, you make him lose energy. That's why the oppressor needs to be insulted. He should not be pitied.

*— I was always afraid to manifest agression. I always wanted to do that, but I was always afraid. By the way, I recalled our reaction in Israel. We got scared when we saw a girl on the street being beaten. But she was not scared. She was saying, "Give me more! Give me more!"*

— This is a consciousness shift.

*— I can't hit her. I am scared.*

— You need to transfer yourself into a different state. You need to get excited. She started to apply psychological pressure on you right away. You must do the same. Speak up. Keep talking about your states.

*— I feel a lot of hatred! I want to kill her!*

— Alina, you have to let it out! You have a lot of hatred saved in you, too.

*— I want to defend myself.*

— No. You must move into the offensive side. You must accuse her. She is guilty. She knows she is guilty, but you don't know that.

*— Did you hurt your younger sister when you were kids? You did! Did you force her to sing songs? You did! Do you know what this little sister of yours wants to do to you for the rest of her life? She wants to kill you. She wants you to feel what she felt! She wants you to feel as powerless as she was back then. You are standing there, and you cannot do anything. Imagine, you are standing there, and you cannot hit her back.*

*— Do you think your sister liked that? Do you think she recalls what you did to her with a smile? No! She hates you! I feel it! I've just felt it! Oh, I'm shivering!*

— Great! Alina, you did great! This is how this shift to the oppressor occurs. And there is an equally strong victim there. Boom, and you shift from one into another. A minute passes and you are back into the victim. All these cocky bastards are equally cowardly. And neither side is bad; this is simple mechanics. Behind the fear of being beaten is the desire to beat someone. But this must be experienced and thoroughly felt. When it gets stuck and does not manifest itself, you live in fear.

— *I experience collossal excitation when I am in the oppressor, but when I move into the victim, it disappears.*

## If you are the victim on the conscious side, you are an oppressor on the subconscious side

— She almost never gets into the oppressor, but oppressors are next to her all the time. She was given a conscious program of the side of the victim. But on a sub-conscious level, she carries the opposite side—the oppressor. This side must be opened.

— *It has to be opened in order for her to stop subconsciously oppressing other people.*

— *I was almost raped as a young girl. I went to a club, and there was this situation there, but he was unable to pull off my jeans.*

— *You can't even experience being a victim normally!*

— *I was crazy when I was young. I got in a car with a man by myself. I asked him to give me a lift. He tried to get under my skirt, but I knocked him down.*

— There is a good manual on how to fight the aggressors I can lend you. It starts like this: "You find a busy street. You find a good, strong oppressor. You hit him on the head with a stick. Then you kick him in the groin. He goes down. You jump him and start kicking him with your feet. When you confirm he is not breathing, you start looking for another oppressor."

— *I cannot watch movies depicting animals being killed.*

— *I cannot pass a stray cat easily. I think this is one of my own projections.*

— *I can start crying while watching a cartoon.*

— All of you are far from the neutral position.

*— A street dog was run over by a car in front of my house a few months ago. I took him to the vet, but he died anyway. I was very upset. I cried for weeks.*

*— In my case, it is different. My cats keep dying on me. I get a new cat, but a week or two later it is dead. It gets killed by a dog or it falls from a roof. I can't understand that.*

— They take your karma. Your karma is so big that one cat is not enough.

*— What kind of patience should one have? I would not get another cat if one were to die on me tomorrow.*

— It has nothing to do with patience. She either has to die herself or her cat should die. You are quite far from wholeness, as we can see.

*— What does it mean to get to "zero" in this particular duality? Will it happen when one is calm in either role: in the role of an oppressor and in the role of a victim?*

**— You will get to "zero" when you stop being attracted by these roles. Try to understand, if you are afraid of being beaten up, you will attract a situation where you will be beaten up. If you are afraid of being insulted, you will attract a corresponding situation. You realize your fear.**

*— Hmmm, nobody beat me after this situation. I was only beaten morally since.*

## How do opposite poles attract each other?

— It means you are morally afraid. You scream, "How can you hurt a little girl?!" Who else can we hurt here? We can only hurt those who are weaker than us. Try to see how you create this field. Everyone is trying to attract money, but not you. You have learned how to attract the oppressor. Until you have played this game out, you will continue to play it. And you play this game well. You play it very well. You cry! You are playing it for real. You are crying and screaming, "Hit me! Hit me!" The oppressor has done everything he could. The oppressor is tired already, but he cannot pass you by when you are asking for more.

— *I used to scream, yell, and fight as a kid. That was my way to express my emotions. But one day, someone told me that I look ugly when I scream, and that was it. I could not do it again.*

— *One of the boys in my elementary school called me fat, and I was unable to eat anything sweet ever since. I used to look at myself in the mirror thinking, "Am I fat or not?"*

— *Svetlana keeps bringing up stories from our childhood. She claims I used to get her upset. I am four years older. I don't remember her at all.*

— *She is still looking up to you.*

— *Right now, when I was observing the fight between the two of them, I felt real horror. For me, oppression is connected to the state of not being free. It looks like freedom is very important for me. I just saw it as a reason for my being alone. The state of not being free scares and repels me.*

— Take a look at how not free I am. I have to come here every day and listen to your stories. Imagine how not free I am.

— *Well, we go to work every day, too.*

— I don't even go to work. I spend all my time with you.

— *I am also afraid. I am afraid I will be prevented from doing what I want and living the way I want.*

— "I don't know how I want to live, but don't prevent me from living the way I want!"

— *Yes. Don't get in my way! Let it be difficult and bad, but I want to do it myself.*

— I will reject everything I am offered.

— *I get very angry when my husband calls and asks me where I am.*

— What about love?

— *How is it connected?*

194

— What do you mean? Where can he find you? He wants to come and kiss you. He wants to bring you flowers, and you reply, "Go to hell! Don't impinge on my freedom." He says, "I love you!" You reply, "Get lost!"

— *There is this guy who used to work with me. He keeps sending me text messages asking me to marry him. I got so irritated once, and I told him to fuck off.*

— That was a mistake. This is the love you are looking for. This is your love part.

— *I have a question. We talked yestedray about victim, oppressor, and their "plus" and "minus" poles. The way I understand this is that we have to play both the victim and oppressor roles, and we have to play both of these roles in "plus" and "minus" poles.*

— That's right. The oppressor has a "plus" pole and a "minus" pole, and a victim has a "plus" pole and a "minus" pole. Until you see all four of them and balance them, you will be of center.

— *Do we have to experience all four of them and start to feel and understand when each one of them gets turned on?*

— You have to experience your victim with plus and with minus, and you have to experience your oppressor with plus and with minus. The victim has her plus, too. You have trouble seeing this plus.

— *So, do I have to see these four positions in every situation that I try to sort out? Do I have to see these positions in myself and in my part represented externally: two in me and two in my part?*

— *I have noticed that when I get in a totally crazy situation and when my mental center does not understand anything, the only remedy is self-investigation. This process distracts me from the crazy states I am in, and as I sort things out, I get out of them. While I try to sort out who is the oppressor and who is the victim here … My boyfriend asked me, "Why do you only believe your Pint? Why don't you believe me?" I explained to him that your knowledge puts everything in the right place in my head. I finally sorted out what is what and who*

195

*is who in this world. I have not experienced everything we have discussed, but theoretically, I have started to understand what is going on. I've read many smart books and visited quite a few psychologists, but it was your knowledge that opened my eyes. I don't need to believe. I know that this is it.*

*— I went through some crazy times, seeing some of my thoughts instantly reflected in the external world. When I had chaos in my head and could not make a decision, I would instantly see it in the external world. And I understood that I had to sort things out inside my head first. When I start to see my parts and try to come to truce with them, I may receive a phone call for example, that situation has been resolved.*

*— Yes. I have experienced this external confirmation of my internal state many times. I used to explore the external world. Now I spend more time in my inner world.*

— According to your faith, be it unto you.

*— A am greatful to you, Alexander Alexandrovich, for sharing this knowledge with us. Thank you for what you do.*

— Finally, someone has expressed something positive. Finally, someone said thank you.

*— Thank you, Alexander Alexandrovich!*

www.ingramcontent.com/pod-product-compliance
Lightning Source LLC
Chambersburg PA
CBHW072137270326
41931CB00010B/1791

9 781944 722067